AT SEA IN THE CITY

At Sea in the City

NEW YORK FROM THE WATER'S EDGE

❦

by William Kornblum

with a foreword by Pete Hamill

illustrations by Oliver Williams

ALGONQUIN BOOKS
OF CHAPEL HILL
2002

Published by
ALGONQUIN BOOKS OF CHAPEL HILL
Post Office Box 2225
Chapel Hill, North Carolina 27515-2225

a division of
Workman Publishing
708 Broadway
New York, New York 10003

Library of Congress Cataloging-in-Publication Data
Kornblum, William.
    At sea in the city : New York from the water's edge /
by William Kornblum.
        p. cm.
    Includes bibliographical references.
    ISBN 1-56512-265-8
    1. New York (N.Y.)—Description and travel.   2. New York (N.Y.)—
History.   3. Kornblum, William—Journeys—New York (State)—New
York.   4. Sailing—New York (State)—New York.   5. Waterways—
New York (State)—New York.   I. Title.
F128.55 .K67 2002
974.7'1—dc21   2002018306

10 9 8 7 6 5 4 3 2 1
First Edition

For Noah, Eve, and Johanna

CONTENTS

Acknowledgments ix

Foreword xi

Introduction 1

1 HOME WATERS *13*

2 UP ON THE ROLLING SEA *33*

3 JAMAICA BAY, GATEWAY *61*

4 INTO THE NARROWS *99*

5 CONCRETE *135*

6 EAST RIVER PASSAGE *159*

7 THE HELL GATE *183*

8 AT THE THROGS NECK *205*

Epilogue 225

Bibliography 229

Acknowledgments

I'LL NEVER ADEQUATELY THANK all the friends and colleagues who made this book so enjoyable to live and to write. I fear that any listing would be partial at best. My real dream is to take everyone sailing, and with time and some luck, Susan and I may accomplish that happy feat. For now, let me formally thank the people from Algonquin Books. Editor Duncan Murrell picked out this manuscript from the unsolicited pile and showed me how to realize my hopes for it. Elisabeth Scharlatt, Algonquin's publisher, was the most creative and professional book adviser a writer could ask for. Thanks also to Elisabeth's staff: Lynn Strong, copy editor; Dana Stamey, managing editor; Anne Winslow, designer; and Craig Popelars, marketing director. Finally, mapmaker and Yankee fan Oliver Williams was a joy to work with, especially during the 2001 World Series.

My family members were the earliest, if most biased, believers in this book. Eve read passages to friends and convinced me to put it out in the world. Noah and Johanna gave me endless encouragement and never hesitated to come sailing. Susan lived every moment of it with me, which was the greatest blessing, and since our sailing adventures continue, it still is.

Foreword

I'm a New Yorker, born and bred, and have lived most of my life in the company of rivers and the sea. Each day of my childhood in a top floor flat of a Brooklyn tenement, I could see the harbor. Sometimes the windows were rimed with winter ice. Sometimes they were open to sultry August. But there was the harbor, with the Statue of Liberty like a green toy and the skyline off to the right and Staten Island and New Jersey reduced to distant brown smears. From those windows, and from our rooftops, we could see the troopships coming home after the war had ended in Europe, while foghorns issued baritone announcements of triumph, and ten thousand church bells pealed, and the people on those rooftops roared their welcome. Look, there's the *Queen Mary*. And that ship, the white one, what is that?

After all the young men were home, embraced on our piers by those who loved them, and then dispersed through our city and throughout the United States, we saw the ships of peace: dark muscular freighters, immense ocean liners, all nudged and shoved and guided through the channels by what seemed to be hundreds of tough, ropy little tugboats. The harbor was always dense with movement. We all knew that we lived in a port.

But there were other currents moving in our young lives, and they were about more than simple geography. My parents were immigrants from Belfast, in Northern Ireland, and my mother's father, Peter Devlin, was a man who went to sea. My sister still has some of his papers, sketching distant journeys to Rangoon and Yokohama through the distant seas of Joseph Conrad. Peter Devlin rose to become an engineer for the Great White Fleet, charged with hauling bananas from Central America to the tables of Europe. When he married and had two children, he decided it was time to leave the sea and settled in Brooklyn to work for the Cunard Line. There, in 1916, when my mother was five, he was killed in an accident. His small family returned to Ireland. But my mother never could escape the pull of New York.

And so she helped us see New York for what it was then: a city of rivers and bridges and a great welcoming harbor. From our rooftop, she could see the place where her father died. She could see Ellis Island, too, and the spires of Manhattan. She saw all of this with an immigrant's sense of pure human wonder, and she passed it to us. Her tutelage was not a matter of mere words. She took us—my brother Tom, my sister Kathleen—on long walks. On some days, we walked upon the Brooklyn Bridge high over the East River, while she explained that it wasn't really a river at all, it was an estuary, and the water flowed south and north at the same time, uptown and down.

Way up there at the top of the estuary, she said, there was a place called Hell Gate where old wooden ships were smashed into splinters. And she loved that bridge itself. For us, it was an astonishment, soaring, sweeping, its cables singing in the wind, put there by amazing men.

The bridge led us into lower Manhattan, and our wanderings took many directions. Sometimes we went to the Battery to look out upon the immensity of the harbor. During the American Revolution, the harbor had frozen solid, and British cavalry crossed the ice with horses and cannon, trying to finish off George Washington. He would live to see the British sail away forever on November 25, 1783, waiting high in the ruined city until word came that the last ship had sailed. Then Washington led his battered, injured, and triumphant army in the first great parade in our history. For almost a century, the event was celebrated as Evacuation Day. And right there, said my mother, pointing at St. Paul's Chapel on Broadway and Fulton Street: right there George Washington went to pray.

On some days, we would take the subway to Times Square and walk west to see the ruined hulk of a liner called the *Normandie*. It had burned at its pier in February 1942, and there were dark rumors of Nazi sabotage, which appealed to my melodramatic imagination. I was then six. The once luxurious liner lay on its side like some immense wounded sea creature, and we asked my mother, over and over again, to go to see the *Normandie,* and over and over again she took us, in good weather and bad. Burners and welders worked over the hulk, taking it apart for scrap. Each time we saw her, there was less of her. Today, when I think about wartime New York, I still see the *Normandie*.

As a young man, I went to work as a reporter for the *New York Post*, which was then at 75 West Street, across the street from those United Fruit piers. The *Post* was an afternoon newspaper, and it was believed that afternoon papers must be located along the rivers, south of Canal Street. From such bases, they could avoid midtown traffic by using the great bridges to race to the boroughs with their early editions. Up the street from the *Post* was the *New York World-Telegram & Sun*, where Joseph Mitchell (mentioned fondly in this book) worked alongside A. J. Liebling and H. Allen Smith in the years before the war. Mitchell's pieces for the *New Yorker* thrilled most newspapermen and were filled with deep, loving knowledge of our many waters. He was from North Carolina, not New York, but from his daily labors on our waterfront, he put New York deep in his bones.

I usually worked nights, still known then as the "lobster shift," and when the shift ended at eight in the morning, I set out with a few hollow-eyed colleagues in search of food. Usually we went to Sloppy Louie's, around "the horn" (as we called the tip of Manhattan) on South Street, facing the East River. The old-timers still called the Hudson the "North River," a tradition dating back to the seventeenth-century Dutch (the South River was in Maryland). So the North River was on the west side of Manhattan, and South Street was on the east side, and all of it made absolute sense over fresh fish and mugs of beer.

In those days there was still a beat called "Shipping News." At five in the morning a gang of reporters and photographers would set out on a launch, bound for an arriving liner parked in quarantine at the Ambrose Lightship. The light was almost always mauve as the sun struggled to rise out of Brooklyn. I loved the way the launch bounced and skidded down the river and into the open harbor, heading for the Narrows (in a year before they built the Verrazano Bridge). Over to the right was Hoboken, where Marlon Brando, Elia Kazan, and Budd Schulberg had made their New York movie masterpiece, *On the Waterfront*. Dead ahead was the Statue of Liberty. Behind us, the skyline, an amazing accident described once by Truman Capote as "a diamond iceberg."

Then we'd be bobbing alongside the hull of the ship and stepping out to take a ladder to the deck. The photographers were charged with immortalizing some celebrity: the Duke of Windsor and his wife or some actress showing her legs on a deck rail. But they had another goal, too. I saw this on my first day on shipping news. I moved up the ladder, made it to the deck, and suddenly was engulfed in a stampede. Some of the photographers still used big Speed Graphics and wore press cards in their hatbands, and they pushed and shoved and hammered me aside. I thought: who could it be? Who is the object of their journalistic passion? Greta Garbo? Jayne Mansfield? Dwight Eisenhower?

It was the food. They slammed through the doors into the dining room, where an immense feast awaited them. Hosted by elegant stewards. Complete with wine or beer.

In 1962, the first nonstop jet airliners began flying to Europe. Within a few years, the transatlantic passenger lines were dying. The longshoremen and stevedores found other work. The old saloons closed their doors. Nobody went out on shipping news anymore. Around the time of Jack Kennedy's assassination, the North River began to die. The Port Authority of New York and New Jersey—charged with maintaining the health of the port—decided that the situation was without hope and went into the real estate business. They would build the World Trade Center, featuring the tallest towers in the world. The final remnant of the Washington Market was closed. Cortlandt Street was bulldozed into history. The United Fruit piers soon vanished. As land was cleared for the new development, the rubble removed from its deep foundations was moved across West Street to be used as landfill that would eventually become Battery Park City. The watery world I knew as a boy was vanishing before me.

And yet, while reading this fine book, I was reminded of several things. One is my own ignorance. The book is filled with detailed explorations of the shoreline and waters of a world I had almost always seen from land and did not truly know. As one example: I had romped through many weekends, man and boy, on the sands of Coney Island, and loved the paintings of Reginald Marsh and David Levine that captured so much of its rowdy essence. Mr. Kornblum has helped me see that piece of New York with fresh eyes. I had flown over Jamaica Bay many times, had even covered the discovery of a few gangland corpses in its marshes. But here it comes vividly to life in a different way. On page after page, I've learned something new.

The other thing it suggested to me is a belief in a certain hard-boiled optimism. It is easy in our world to throw hands in the air and walk away, convinced that nothing will ever get better. But here, starting with Mr. Kornblum himself, we meet people who refuse to surrender. They work to repair damage. They insist on leaving the world better than it was when they found it. They understand that the natural world is the property of all of us, and we must honor it, too.

For several millennia, rivers have been used as symbols of time, the flowing waters passing through our fingertips as swiftly as the seconds of our lives. Here Mr. Kornblum captures the sense of past, present, and future that abides in the waters of New York. Even the mightiest buildings come and go. Ships are launched and end up in scrapyards. Famous names fade into obscurity. But there are the rivers. There is the harbor. They will be here long after all of us are gone.

Pete Hamill

AT SEA IN THE CITY

Introduction

*M*y family and I have been sailing the waters of the city for twenty years. On an adventurous cruise, we sail through the Narrows, up the East River, out to Long Island Sound, and then reverse course some days later to return through East Rockaway Inlet to our home port of Long Beach. On our voyages into the New York harbor, there is always some new discovery to be made.

With all its congestion and crowding, and after the ignorant damage three centuries of commerce and industry inflicted on its wetlands and waterways, New York City would seem the last place to undertake a voyage of discovery. Over the past three decades or more, the waters, wetlands, shorelines, and green spaces of the metropolitan region have actually improved. Immense new sewage treatment plants have largely eliminated raw sewage from the waters, and in consequence fewer beaches are closed due to fecal coliform pollution. The most destructive pesticides have been banned, and more birds of all kinds are nesting and reproducing in urban habitats. New Yorkers have gained a new appreciation of the need to preserve and restore natural habitats within the city, and more varieties of fishes and birds are returning to the city, the result of decades of fitful progress, end-less meetings, and self-sacrificing efforts by nameless and well-known people alike.

The sailing and coastal explorations I describe in this book occurred during the warm months of the last decades of the century, and most of them since 1997—trips with friends and family from my home in Long Beach, through some of the city's waterways and out into Long Island Sound. The voyages took us to all five boroughs and then some, with inevitable exploratory digressions and emergency diversions.

The dream of making these voyages, and the idea that I could try to make the waters of my own city into my home waters, formed in my mind during a weekend on the beaches of Cape Cod, long ago in my youth. Before falling asleep one night, I had read a paragraph by Thoreau in which he observed that a person would have to be a genius to fully know the way from "the front door to the path." I awoke with the sun the next morning still thinking about the many possible meanings of the passage.

In 1855, when Thoreau tramped the beaches of Cape Cod, he noted everywhere the effects of human commerce and industry. His journal records with fascinating detail the varieties of flotsam he saw washing up on the beaches. Shortly before he began his long walk from Eastham to Provincetown, a passenger ferry and freighter were sunk with the loss of many lives: "A little further along the shore we saw a man's clothes on a rock; further, a woman's scarf, a gown, a straw bonnet, the brig's caboose, and one of her masts high and dry, broken into several pieces."

Stunned by the power of the ocean, Thoreau noted that "the largest timbers and iron pieces were broken superfluously, and I saw that no material could withstand the power of the waves."

When he made his visit, Cape Cod was "wholly unknown to the fashionable world." He knew that "the time must come when this coast will be a place of resort for those New Englanders who really wish to visit the seaside," but he was also confident that fashion would never spoil the Outer Cape: "Such beaches as are fashionable are here made and unmade in a day, I may almost say, by the sea shifting its sands. A storm in the fall or winter is the time to visit it . . . a lighthouse or a fisherman's hut the true hotel. A man may stand there and put all America behind him."

But even as he was snugly holed up with the keeper of the Highland Light at North Truro, wondering still at the drama of nature and man in the "wild, rank place, with no flattery in it," Thoreau found out that he and his traveling companion were momentary suspects in a bank robbery that had just taken place to the north in Provincetown. Urban America was already catching up to them.

The city had begun to shape the life of that lonely barrier beach in ways that were quite evident to observers like Thoreau. All along the beach lay strewn the detritus of a bustling commercial civilization: dead horses and cattle, garbage from the lumbering sailing freighters, beams and pilings from far-off docks and sunken ships, bits of clothing, the washed-up carcass of a dead whale, its blubber stripped far out at sea, tossed up on the sand for its bones to be picked clean by creatures of every phylum. The expanse of sand and dunes and sea was so great that it seemed to absorb all traces of human activity along the tide line. There was plenty of room for foxes and beavers. Flights of shorebirds darkened the sky during times of migration. But some of the people of the beaches hoped to snare whatever human bounty the sea might toss ashore. They were known as "wreckers" then, and with sand sledges and crude wooden carts they salvaged beams and twisted ironwork, or cut the splintered planks into firewood for sale to the crofters and the lighthouse keepers.

In the lighthouses at Race Point and elsewhere on the Outer Cape, as at Fire Island and Sandy Hook, solitary keepers stood vigil year-round in the sweep of nature. Their task was to see to it that the lights burned to warn off the ships that otherwise might spill their cargoes of people and goods along the wild beach. A man could only imagine that he had turned his back on America; in reality America was even then promising to overwhelm the beaches and the oceans themselves with effluvia.

A century and a half later the coasts have changed. There is the same ebb and flow, the same tides and currents of sand, the same winds and blooms of seaweed and jellyfish. But the coast is almost everywhere a congested and settled strand of sand and roadway with vacationers and natives interspersed in symbiotic roosting. Public beach lands comprise only about 10 percent of the shore here and throughout the United States. The beaches and tidewaters are carved up into a bewildering array of private claims and public jurisdictions.

In the century since Thoreau and other keen observers of the American scene walked the beaches and valleys of our land, there has been a widening division between writing about nature and writing about city life and social matters. Nature writers have their hands full reminding the reading public that there still is a natural world that reveals the great chain of being and other deeper mysteries of life in the biosphere. But inside the city it's easy to think that nature begins somewhere outside our windows.

Beaches and wetlands, whales and striped bass, and birds of all kinds exert powerful influences on our city lives, and we are finally making them part of our political economy. To preserve a habitat for a fish species, the Hudson River striped bass, New Yorkers defeated a massive highway project along Manhattan's Hudson shore. As I write this, New Yorkers are working to restore wetlands wherever they exist, and to create a chain of priceless public parks along the Hudson through midtown Manhattan and along the East River as well. As an urban sociologist and a native New Yorker, I've had the opportunity to work with dedicated activists and professionals all over the United States on the creation of urban national parks and the restoration of irreplaceable park lands. I've also been part of planning efforts to rebuild or enhance many different parks from New York to Cape Cod and other stretches of our endangered shoreline. Wherever my family and I voyaged on the New

York waters, I saw the follies of commercial and industrial development, but from the deck of our sailboat I could also see the stirrings of restoration.

New York is an archipelago with only about one-eighth of the city on the mainland of North America. The boroughs of Brooklyn and Queens are part of Long Island. Manhattan makes New York a world city, but wedged between the Hudson and East Rivers it is an island unto itself; so is Staten Island, separated from New Jersey by the Kill Van Kull and from the Battery by a beautiful ferry ride. Only the Bronx moors the city to the continent.

There are a host of smaller islands in the New York archipelago, some extremely well known like Liberty and Ellis Islands, some less well known like Hoffman and Swinburne in the Narrows, or Shooters and Prall's, the bird sanctuary islands in Kill Van Kull, or the gloomy North and South Brothers across the East River from Rikers, the prison island. New York's waterways were the reason it was once the nation's premier seaport, and with the help of the Erie Canal, which linked the port to the nation's hinterland, they were a major reason for the city's extraordinary growth. All the rivers flowing around the city's islands have freshwater tributaries and thus contain changing mixtures of salt and fresh waters, making this one of the world's foremost urban estuaries. The inland waterways, combined with the city's ocean beaches, give the city a total of 578 miles of shoreline, including about 320 miles of piers and bulkheads.

In the wider world, Manhattan island *is* the city. Relatively few of the city's millions of annual visitors ever get beyond its shores. But even to most native New Yorkers, the small islands or uninhabited islands of the urban archipelago are unknown and mysterious. Almost all of them were places of exile and isolation where sick people or criminals were isolated from the community, and some, Rikers Island most notably, still serve that purpose. Other islands and parts of the shoreline were dedicated to defending the New York harbor from attacks by sea and air; their military history lurks in the remnants of forts, missile bases, naval installations, none of them much used in actual defensive battle. For the more remote islands, residential or commercial development is out of the question, and over the past years they have been colonized by other species, especially the working birds of the harbor.

New Yorkers do have an ongoing love affair with their beaches and wetlands, which wrap the city in ribbons of green marsh and silver sand and are gifts of inestimable value. The surge of city people to ocean beaches during a steamy summer heat wave is one of the earth's notable migrations, greater in scale than the migrations of the Serengeti or Yellowstone. Over a million and a half people stream toward the city's shores on a sultry weekend day in summer. Five subway lines descend on Coney Island, the city's most famous beach strand, but Brighton Beach, Manhattan Beach, and the Rockaway beaches are also accessible by subway for hundreds of thousands of day visitors in the warm months. The Bronx has no ocean beaches, but Orchard Beach in Pelham Bay Park on Long Island Sound draws crowds from the Bronx and Manhattan and is the place to go to see some serious salsa dancing. South Beach and Great Kills on Staten Island are quieter beach parks with inspiring views of the Verrazano-Narrows Bridge and the entrance to the New York harbor. Beyond the city stretch the popular barrier beach islands of Long Beach, Jones Beach, Fire Island, and then the classier Hampton beaches ending at Montauk. Asking New Yorkers what beaches they prefer is a more serious question than one may imagine, like asking them to name their favorite baseball team or Chinese restaurant.

Aside from beach excursions, for the past few generations New Yorkers have been separated from the waters that flow around them. Most don't grow up handling small boats, and fears of pollution and heavy industrial marine traffic have reinforced their resolve to stay off the city's rivers and creeks. The physical city separates them from their natural surroundings: the shoreline was largely inaccessible, even after the decline in shipping and manufacturing in the harbor; the piers are rotted and dangerous, although here and there residents of neighborhoods near abandoned piers have claimed them as recreation spaces; walkways and bike paths along the rivers are discontinuous. There has always been a handful of hardy New Yorkers, mainly from blue-collar backgrounds, who fish in small boats on the city's waters, and intrepid naturalists whose passion for the natural world leads them to take up environmental causes. But accounts of East River shoreline fishing expeditions, or of birding along the Manhattan shore, almost always include semi-comic accounts of crawling through wasted no-man's-lands on the edges of the highways, over treacherous guardrails, and across sagging bulkheads.

New York turned its back on its harbor, its rivers and wetlands, and the wildlife they support. Many of the city's most ambitious residential buildings have been gleaming high-rise condominiums along the Hudson and East Rivers. Apartment buyers have paid mounting prices for views of the city and its waterways, from which they were physically and emotionally separated. The critical details of what was going on beneath the water's surface and at the shorelines were someone else's problem. This was a dangerous turn. On a rapidly urbanizing planet, the biological resilience of major estuaries like the one on which New York is built depend on a well-informed and environmentally active citizenry.

EVEN AT THE NADIR of environmental quality in the 1960s, the region's wetlands and barrier island beaches remained vital habitats. In his classic mid-century *A Natural History of New York City,* John Kieran wrote that "Here on the sands and on the mud flats of the bays and inlets at low tide we find shorebirds of many kinds in abundance during migration and at least a few species at any time of year." Among many examples, Kieran describes the sanderling *(Crocethia alba),* a shorebird that runs in and out of each advancing wave in the spring and summer, not far from clusters of children scampering at the ocean's edge under parents' watchful eyes. The semipalmated sandpiper *(Ereuntes pusillus),* one of four species of sandpipers, also known as "peeps," skims along our beaches and mudflats and may be our most abundant shorebird. Its synchronized darting and dashing at the water's edge enlivens our beaches, as do the flights of geese and ducks, and diving terns, and the mere sight of the dune grasses swaying in the wind.

From a biological perspective, those coastal grasses and black-earth wetlands remain the most precious habitats of our region. In fact, they are the defining ecological feature of the entire American coastline from Cape Cod to Florida and the Gulf of Mexico. The eastern coast slopes gently along the continental shelf to about thirty miles offshore, where it plunges abruptly to depths of hundreds and then thousands of feet in the deep ocean. Sand particles, ground from stone by northern rivers and glaciers, flow in longshore currents and are deposited by the waves onto beaches and sandbars along our coasts. In recent geological time, in the twelve thousand years since the last ice age, these sand deposits along the ocean shores have become dune-crested barrier islands, behind which arose quiet lagoons and inlets like Great South Bay, the Peconics, Raritan Bay, Barnegat Bay, the great Chesapeake, and many, many more. The region's tidal lagoons are where some of our favorite fish species, especially those in the flounder family, breed and begin their seaward migrations. The marsh grasses nourish a chain of creatures on which our magnificent shorebirds depend.

All the early observers of our coasts were struck by the teeming riches of the coastal wetlands, the rich oyster and clam beds, the flights of birds darkening the sky, but they were also appalled by their "green monotony." The wetlands were so extensive that it seemed of no consequence to immediately begin draining and filling them for human "improvement." The race to make them into real estate continues, so that today about 50 percent of the original marshes in the coastal United States have been destroyed, most before we began to fully understand their importance in the great chain of being. It may already be too late to save our coastlines from the consequences of human growth and ignorance, but as I write, more and more New Yorkers are insisting that the city reclaim its shoreline for public use. Fitfully, New Yorkers are seeking to understand and, where possible, to restore a patrimony they almost entirely wasted.

When Walt Whitman wandered the beaches of Long Island and crossed the East River on the Brooklyn ferry in the years before the Civil War, New York was a bustling seaport city. Many would argue that it still is, and on sunset walks along the beach near my home it is routine to see eight or more freighters waiting for the tide to shift before moving into the Ambrose Channel for a passage into the city. There are millions of tons of cargo handled in the harbor, most of it loaded on and off in containers in the highly automated New Jersey freight ports. But compared to what they were in Whitman's day, the rivers and bays are ghostly. Even when I was growing up in the forties and fifties, the rivers were busy with ship and tug traffic of all kinds. There were thousands of longshoremen and sailors visible in the active port, and that was already at the end of the harbor's peak of activity. Tugs and barges and great ships arrive and depart all the time, but the city's marine traffic and maritime culture are nothing like they once were.

The city's powerful waterways are again undergoing a transition and are becoming a recreation center for people with imagination and time to explore the city's edges. Some of the commercial port activity remains, and new maritime uses need nurturing so that the harbor won't lose its economic vitality. The old industrial neighborhoods and their shorelines are attracting young residents who are joining with older neighborhood activists to restore shorelines and public access to the water. This change is occurring as I write: the Hudson River park system, the Brooklyn waterfront park system, and other public-access projects along our rivers are well under way. Nature study, especially birding, is one of the fastest-growing forms of recreation in the city. Community groups and some city leaders are encouraging boating, fishing, use of the shoreline by artists, and a host of activities that make city residents more aware of the special qualities of their environment.

But most of the planning for our waterfront focuses on the land-bound pedestrian and park visitors, or on the possibilities of ferry transit for commuters. There are few places along the rivers to tie up small boats and fewer places to take on passengers. In time that will change, as adventurous people in kayaks, canoes, rowboats, and sailing vessels of all description continue in ever-expanding numbers to explore the urban archipelago. This book is, in part, an appreciation of the city as seen from the water.

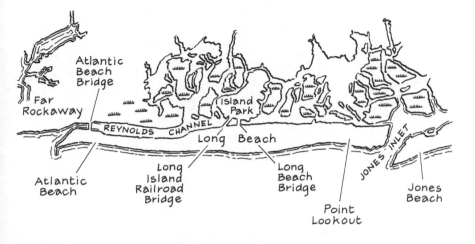

ATLANTIC   OCEAN

1 / *Home Waters*

> They sailed away in a sieve, they did,
> In a sieve they sailed so fast,
> With only a beautiful pea-green veil
> Tied with a riband by way of a sail,
> To a small tobacco pipe mast . . .
>
> —Edward Lear, "The Jumblies"

*T*he vessel we sailed on our New York voyages was named *Tradition*. This was the name she was given in 1910, when she was launched at the Crosby boatyards in Osterville on Cape Cod. She was a worn-out twenty-four-foot New England catboat, built by the most famous maker of these boats at a time when they were the most common all-purpose work and pleasure craft along the shallow barrier island bays and inlets of our northern coasts and estuaries.

Tradition carried a single huge mainsail on her wooden spars. The sail was rigged with wooden hoops to her stout, ancient mast, dark with the stains of time and the sea, and laced to a boom that extended aft some twenty-five feet from the mast near the bow, beyond the sturdy wheel and beyond the boat's transom. The sail was hauled aloft by a wooden gaff to which was connected an efficient system of halyards and blocks. A throat halyard pulled up the gaff by its throat, while the two jaws moved up along the mast, and there was a peak halyard that lifted the aft portions of the sail. A third halyard, the topping lift, raised the boom, in part so this formidable club could swing safely over the heads of crew and passengers when the boat was tacking through the wind. All the halyards ran from the mast to the boat's ample cockpit, and the sail could be raised or lowered by a single sailor without having to run forward to manage the sails, as is the case with most modern sailing rigs.

Catboats passed out of favor among yachting people in the early decades of the twentieth century. They were replaced by the graceful sloops whose shortened mainsails and higher-reaching Marconi (triangular peaked) sails and forward jibs could add speed in lighter breezes, and whose heeling in the wind gives a greater impression of speed than the more upright and beamy cat.

The working catboats of Cape Cod, Great South Bay and Barnegat Bay were good all-purpose boats for tending fishing nets and for use as charter fishing boats on the weekends. A classic Currier and Ives print from the turn of the nineteenth century shows a catboat and its captain carrying intent young men and laughing women trolling for bluefish in a choppy ocean inlet. Generations of fishermen and local boatbuilders refined the catboat for heavy work along the coasts. But as the fishermen discovered motors that could carry them out of calms or squalls, the slower-sailing cats held less appeal for men whose livelihoods depended on getting the catch to market as fast as possible, and who would also prefer to get to the dinner table sooner and with more certainty. Many old fishing catboats lost their masts and sails and puttered along for years as motorized fishing boats.

But catboats are well evolved for sailing over our particular shoals, and they turn out to be extraordinarily adaptable to contemporary life on the waters of the East Coast cities. Like a whale's body, the shape of a boat's hull and the arrangement of its rigging are evolutionary solutions to complex problems of life in particular marine surroundings. "The one essential factor in the design of boats proven by history," wrote maritime historian Howard Chappel, "is that they must fit the conditions where they are used and for what they are used. . . . No one sits down and tries to figure out how to build a boat that is all round 'better.' He tries to figure out, instead, how to fit an existing boat so that she will do better the work for which she is required. This was certainly the case with the commercial catboat."

It may no longer be well adapted for sport or commercial fishing, but the catboat was still ideal for family voyages. *Tradition* was small enough for one sailor to handle and relatively easy on a strained household budget. Her four-cylinder gas engine burned about fifty dollars worth of gasoline a season, from April to late October or November. Her eleven-foot width sat flat on the water; her great beam made her extremely accommodating. You couldn't stand in the cabin below, and every boating season began with at least one sharp knock on the head, but there was plenty of room below for a huge double berth, a small galley, a portable marine head, a long bookshelf, and assorted storage nooks. On deck there was room for ten people to go on a day's outing without feeling crowded. When they were young, our children slept under the stars on *Tradition*'s broad deckhouse.

SUSAN AND I BEGAN SAILING small boats together in 1963 when we were Peace Corps volunteers on the west coast of Africa, on the Ivory Coast. I lived in a tribal fishing village on the outskirts of the capital, Abidjan, where I taught physics and chemistry at the Lycée Classique d'Abidjan. Susan lived an hour outside the city in a small college town, where she taught math.

Wandering along the beach outside the city one day, I spotted the rotting hulk of an open-decked sloop, draped it over the back of a rented truck, and hauled it back to a local lagoon. A village carpenter made the major repairs. I finished the boat and rigged it for sailing. On its maiden voyage, two African friends from my village took the chance of being the first to go out with me. A crowd of curious villagers lined the beach. (Their preferred watercraft was a sleek dugout canoe with a good fifteen horse Johnson outboard.) We sailed off smartly, and I took a few tacks through the wind. Heading back to shore to pick up Susan for her turn, I forgot to raise the dagger board. The boat hit the bottom and rolled all three of us into about three feet of lagoon water. The entire village erupted in howls. Susan was in stitches.

She hardly understood how little about sailing I actually knew. But always game, she came out with me and we sailed through some splendid tidal estuaries in the Ebrie Lagoon, behind the great ocean beaches. Seventeen years later, when we were settled in Long Beach on another estuary, I managed to get us out on the water again.

Before I bought *Tradition,* Susan teased me by saying, "If you've got to buy another boat, just make sure it doesn't end up in the backyard like the last one." The last one, a battered rowing skiff, had rotted in our yard, proof I was probably not suited to taking proper care of a boat. Still I pored over boat ads in the penny-savers. I had sailed a strong open-decked catboat as a boy on family vacations in Maine with two old salts who gave me lessons. Now and then one of the modern fiberglass catboats would appear in the used boat ads, but they were always far too expensive for us.

TRADITION WAS LYING IN pieces in the back of her seller's cottage when we first set eyes on her. My son, Noah, and I had driven at the crack of dawn to Southold, on the north fork of Long Island, the day after we spotted the ad for her: "1910 Crosby Catboat, hull fiberglassed, engine, $2,500." The owner had assured me over the phone that the boat had been restored and that she was well worth taking a look at. It was 1979, and my father lay dying in Mt. Sinai hospital in Manhattan. I needed a lift. But as Noah and I surveyed *Tradition*'s forlorn condition, settled into the lawn of a Southold backyard, under a ragged canvas cover, it was hard to know what to think. Her lines, her sturdiness, her ample deck and cockpit space, her wooden spars, and all the rest were evident. She was traditional, all right, but modified over the years and now facing an uncertain future, perhaps only as another backyard compost pile.

My heart was beating wildly with the sudden panic of a man about to act like a boy by making an impulse purchase. I could hear all the voices of experience and reason telling me to get another opinion, shop around, try for a better price. Noah and I took a walk down Southold's Main Street and thought it over. *Tradition*'s owner guaranteed that the engine had worked the last time the boat was in the water but did not say when that actually was. The prop turned easily, suggesting that the engine was not beyond hope, but the wiring looked abysmal. The modern Dacron sail was in good shape, however, and with its great size, that was important; a new one would cost almost the price of the boat itself. I could feel myself letting go. The beauty of the lines, the sheer breadth of her, the turn of her bilge, and the overhung transom had me. We took deep breaths. I paid the $2,500 asking price minus a token $100, to prove back home that we drove a hard bargain, and then made arrangements to have *Tradition* shipped to a working boatyard near our home on Reynolds Channel.

WHEN HE SAW OUR purchase, Howard Sacken, who in those days ran Sacken's Boatyard with his son Mark, was not pleased. He was downright grumpy.

"This is a piece of shit," he muttered. "Look at that paint flaking off the hull, and those barnacles. You're going to have to take all that down bare before you can even begin to think about trying to fix the place on the keel around the prop where the fiberglass has failed."

We would be lucky, Howard scoffed, if the scow ever made it into the water. Once we got the pieces together and the sweaty scraping done on the hull, etc., he'd have to see what could be done with the engine, which itself was an obsolete affair with a prewar Wisconsin cylinder block and many parts by makers no longer in business. Rewiring was the least of it; first we would have to find out if it would work at all. With my father's life quickly ebbing away, racing cancer cells wilting his body before our eyes, my mother distraught with fear and grief, and the pressures of teaching, research, and writing deadlines gnawing at me, it seemed I had only added another burden to a long list.

But Noah and I were determined: nothing would prevent us from getting *Tradition* in shape and sailing again. The work cleared the mind and reminded me that I was privileged not to have such work as a daily obligation. I stole hours in the early mornings and evenings during the week and put in some full days on the weekends. We sanded and scraped until we thought our arms would fall off. We showed Howard Sacken and the other salts that we were game. We pestered to have the wiring and other mechanical work done. We read and reread the advice in the marvelous journal of the Catboat Association. But as the weeks dragged by we worried that the craft might never measure up to our dreams. I took on additional research projects and wrote even more reports to pay the yard bills. We withstood the gentle teasing of Susan and Noah's sisters Eve and Johanna, and at times we coaxed them into chipping and painting with us. Howard Sacken could be tired, distracted and loath to explain how the work should proceed. But on good days, when he was not exhausted from the killing pace of labor in a family boat-yard, or when he was not too exasperated by customers who ran their new boats into pilings or burned out their engines need-lessly, he advised us on the nautical arts and crafts.

When we finally launched the boat, it was the end of the 1980 sailing season, but we were so excited to have her in the water that we continued taking her out for short ventures until Thanksgiving. We sailed her up and down Reynolds Channel in some heavy fall wind to test her strength. We soon learned what a wonderful boat she was, but we also learned a good deal about her idiosyncrasies and faults.

Tradition was slow. In a stiff breeze she could keep up with any sailboat her size and some even larger, but in lighter air she tended to flounder in the propeller wash of the powerboats that ripped through the channel. In a strong breeze she scooted along, even pointed well into the wind, but when the wind kicked up above twelve knots her immense sail required short-ening, or reefing, immediately. Reefing a huge catboat sail can be a challenge. Her graceful boom reaching out beyond the stern was a fearsome opponent, capable of rewarding the careless sailor with a good crack on the head. Yet I was happy: I was after the benefits of slowing down and taking a longer look at things, and while *Tradition* got us to our destination under most conditions of seas and wind, she would not be hurried and we had to respect her limits.

There is a picture I treasure in *The Catboat Book,* a collection of articles about the history and care of these boats. The photo features Wilton Crosby's work crew at the turn of the nineteenth century, a decade before they built *Tradition.* The seven workers, including Wilton Crosby of the famous Osterville boat-building family, pose in full sunlight before the open boathouse. They stand impassive, each holding some tools of the trade and looking as if he'd been caught on his way to a more serious task, all but Wilton Crosby wearing a worker's apron.

Wilton Crosby is older than the others. He stares away from the camera, perhaps at one of his creations bobbing with the tide in Osterville Harbor. Surely those men could not have imagined building anything but a capable, honest boat. But wooden boats, no matter how proud their craftsmen were of their skills, cannot last forever, nor did the Crosby brothers presume that they would. Still, these versatile small boats often became such cherished members of their families that they were coddled and nursed into a finicky old age. *Tradition,* built in 1910, ranked as the fifteenth oldest of the original wooden catboats still afloat, most of them built by the Crosbys.

Despite her pedigree, *Tradition* was impure. Only her beautiful lines, her shape in and out of the water, and the pleasing configuration of her spars and rigging were original; she was really more of an idea than the physical embodiment of her Yankee history. Her hull and decks bore a thick fiberglass hide, covering the original wooden beams and planks, rotted and sistered here and there. The fiberglass coating was laid on years before by people who knew what they were doing. She must have been close to firewood when the work was done, because her centerboard was replaced with a three-and-a-half-foot steel keel that bolted through the hull and was a permanent addition to her underwater profile.

On the South Shore of Long Island a fixed keel is an almost fatal flaw for a wide, shallow boat like *Tradition,* a flaw that counteracts the best qualities of such craft. With a retractable centerboard the catboat draws less than two or three feet of water, which means she is ideal for shoal waters on the bays and estuaries of the East Coast, able to run up on a beach at low tide and be lifted off by the flood tide with no difficulty. When she bumps against the bottom, you simply retract her centerboard and float away. *Tradition* had lost that versatility. She could get stuck on the bottom in four feet of water, and if the tide was high when she ran aground, she and her crew spent much extra time on the bay. Her prosthesis also did nothing for her sailing qualities. With a strong breeze over her beam, she bent into the wind with her sail full and her rigging creaking reassuringly. With a following wind nudging her from a hind quarter and her boom payed out, the gusts twisted her around that keel a bit and she wanted to get her nose into the wind, which may not have been a convenient direction, especially in a narrow channel. This weather helm, as it is known, is a problem of the catboat breed, but *Tradition*'s untraditional keel worsened the condition.

Despite those faults she carried our family over the waves for seventeen years and who knows how many other families before ours? After we fixed her up and nursed her into decent condition, *Tradition* let us and our friends see our world from the sea. But only if we were not in a great hurry.

OUT ON BROAD Reynolds Channel, especially if it's a brisk early spring day, a stiff breeze sweeps the marshes and the water. Bright sunshine plays over the swirling current. On such days I liked to head under full sail toward the Atlantic Beach Bridge and then to the ocean beyond. First we'd pass through the opened Long Island Railroad bridge. On the northward shore, by a group of abandoned oil tanks, night heron couples nested in the tortured landscape of matted grasses and construction waste. With luck we might see an adolescent bird picking its way along the rocks and broken pilings there. The usual gang of egrets, herons, cormorants, and ducks mingled with the gulls and terns at the tides' edges. Other birds like the peeps, the willet, and the occasional glossy ibis, in clusters or as single stalkers, poked through the dark banks along Swift Creek.

There is a choice of wetland and urban views on Reynolds Channel. To the south as we headed west for the inlet at the Rockaways, there was the city of Long Beach, and to the north the marshy hummocks and brackish creeks of a precious wetland. The wetlands formed a waving green mat at the back door of the affluent Five Towns.

Long Beach is the urban center of a barrier island. At the island's eastern end is the fishing village of Point Lookout, also a village of building contractors, independent tradesmen, police and fire officers, and summer people from the city. In Point Lookout a person's membership in the village society is measured in generations.

Between Long Beach and Point Lookout lie stretches of town beaches. These are centered around converted beach clubs and the neighborhood of Lido Beach, with expensive private homes near the dunes and bay shores. On the bay side there are a few patches of wetlands that have so far escaped the builders' shovels, in part because they surround a former military missile site. At night lumbering raccoons leave the marshes to fatten themselves at garbage cans, enjoying sumptuous meals of leftovers.

Elephants were brought to the sands of Long Beach in the 1920s to haul pilings for the boardwalk. Later, a strand of swank hotels would stretch along the boardwalk, soon to be replaced by rooming houses, bars, baths, and all the play places that made Long Beach a *station de mer Americaine* in the tradition of shore towns like Coney Island, the Rockaways, and Asbury Park. The speculators and private developers who first built Long Beach had a vision of a "Hollywood by the Sea." They planned the houses after those in Long Beach, California, with Spanish-style stucco and orange tile roofs. Show-business people like Flo Ziegfeld and Fanny Brice spent summers there in houses on the canals.

For all its distinctiveness as a beach resort, the town is also a classic American community with ball fields, bungalows and bars, firehouses, Catholic churches, synagogues of every description, Latinos enough to support three bodegas, a thriving and increasingly integrated center of town with a rich array of churches, a predominantly African-American neighborhood with strong churches and private homes, and a small low-income housing section with attached homes. In the center of town is the restored red brick railroad station, our link with the real city whose towers on clear days fringe the horizon, halfway across the metropolitan region.

Long Beach is also South Shore Long Island, with its own special brand of New York wiseguys, clam bars, and marsh denizens. Halfway down the channel sits a complex of houses with extensive surveillance systems and a fleet of speedboats, a reputed nest of some local crime figures. But most of our neighbors lead far more mundane lives. Not that many ever venture out on the waters.

The winds over Long Beach and the marshes of the South Shore are unpredictable in the spring and fall. The summer wind usually comes off the sea, cutting across the channel at a nice angle to fill a catboat's sails on a beam reach. The wind blows from the grizzled north in the winter at a good angle for making way down the channel, but too cold for sailing. Fall and spring winds are in transition between land and sea currents, often blowing straight down the channel into one's teeth. On many sailing days, however, when the wind blew across *Tradition*'s beam, we reached down Reynolds Channel with no particular destination in mind. We made steady progress on a beam reach, westward along the channel, just enjoying being out on the water and taking stock of the wildlife and local landmarks. One notable structure, about a mile down the channel from Sacken's, is Lindell School, the old red building where Susan and her sisters went to high school. Lindell is now a primary school — a larger high school stands on the channel at the other end of town — but they still play home football games at the old Lindell field. When they were at home, our children would be at the game with their friends, and when they saw us sailing by they would run to the fence along the bay and shout greetings or requests for services to us when we came close to shore.

If Susan was at *Tradition*'s helm, I could sprawl on the cabin deck and watch a football play or two on the field. Invariably, the warm midday sun brought on great lethargy. It was tempting to stare into the sky, letting my mind soar with the lift of the boat and the sight of terns and gulls gliding overhead. Once I watched a formation of Canada geese whisk in at low altitude, under the flight pattern of incoming jets, and remembered Henry Beston's famous avian tribute from *The Outermost House:* "In a world older and more complete than ours they move finished and complete, gifted with extensions of the senses we have lost or never attained, living by voices we shall never hear. They are not brethren, they are not underlings; they are other nations, caught with ourselves in the net of life and time, fellow prisoners of the splendor and travail of the earth."

Lost in such Reynolds Channel reveries one day, I heard a loud CRACK on *Tradition*'s deck. The tide was against us, the air still and soupy. At low throttle, her sail limp, the boat made slow headway past the Cape Cod Colonials, Moorish Revivals, and other bayside villas of Atlantic Beach. Startled by the loud knock, we all looked up at once and saw that a gleaming white object had ricocheted off the boom and was arching against the blue sky.

"That's a golf ball," Eve said, laughing. "It came right past my face and hit the boom."

"Look over there, Dad," Noah called. "Those guys by that house are hitting golf balls at us."

There on the lawn of a magnificent bayfront house was a clutch of slightly paunchy men in bathing suits and even tans. They were holding golf clubs and clapping one of their company on the back, celebrating his perfect stroke. It was a jolly moment for them.

Hot with anger, I gunned the throttle and turned the boat toward their dock. We were a good five-iron away, about a hundred and fifty yards out in the channel. I began shouting at them, and the sound of my anger carried over the still water. Eve and Noah were laughing at the absurdity of it all. Susan tugged at my pants to make me sit down, but I kept up a barrage of gestures and obscenities. As we drew nearer to their dock, the backyard golfers saw that I would not be easily calmed. Their elation turned sour. Sheepishly they turned away from their game and began drifting toward the house, where the women at the gathering were seated on lawn chairs, taking in the full scene.

Tradition took her good time as usual. She was not an ideal attack craft. Or perhaps she was. I could feel my anger dissolving. What would I do at their dock, anyway? Eve had not actually been hit. No one was hurt. Up on the fancy lawn, the fellows now had their backs turned to us. We could smell steaks grilling and hear the whine of a Barry Manilow tune.

"Let's get out of here, Dad," Noah demanded. "These guys are just dorks. They listen to elevator music."

"If they'd hit me in the mouth and busted my braces, we could get some free dental work," Eve added. "There must be at least one orthodontist up there."

"Right full rudder, or whatever," Susan ordered. "We made our point, let's go. They're plenty embarrassed."

As she said this, the one who had made the great shot turned toward us and took some steps in our direction. He held his arms out, palms upturned, as if to say, "Gosh, I'm sorry. Who ever thought I'd actually plunk one right in your tub?" I made a final gesture of my own, a dismissive wave of the arm, and with that we were away, a feature of the scenery that had suddenly disrupted their suburban pastoral before dissolving again into the background.

It is not always quite so absurd out on Reynolds Channel. With a strong spring breeze in her sail, *Tradition* made a more difficult moving target. But there is a good deal of other absurdity to see on our waters. On the weekends, for example, cigarette boats with names like *Exterminator* and *Avenger*, capable of reaching speeds of over forty miles an hour on the water, roar past, their din shattering the afternoon calm. Their passengers sport thick ear protectors so that only the rest of us need be savaged by their racket, and their only saving grace is that they quickly disappear from the waters as dinnertime approaches.

We usually reached the end of Reynolds Channel at the Atlantic Beach Bridge within an hour or two, depending on the tide and strength of the winds. The channel is the seaward path from our dock to the ocean and the New York harbor. On most days we stayed in the channel for a few hours of sailing and fishing, but when we made trips into the city, our arrival at the western end of Long Beach marked only the beginning of an ocean sailing adventure. Fishermen who tied their small boats under the bridge to fish off its pilings for striped bass and blackfish stared at us, a bit of maritime history. Some always looked worried, certain that the mast would crack against the bridge superstructure. But we knew from experience that at any tide *Tradition*'s mast cleared the bridge underspan by at least three feet. Once in the inlet, we scanned the water ahead of us to see where the waves were breaking and whether there were any tugs with heavy-laden oil barges coming in from the ocean across our course. Early in the morning and just before sunset were the best times to head out, when the massive apartment houses of the

Rockaways were silhouetted by shafts of light breaking through the clouds and dancing on the chop. With a steady breeze, *Tradition* moved easily over the waves. No longer hemmed in by the land on either side, she went out of our home waters and up on the rolling sea.

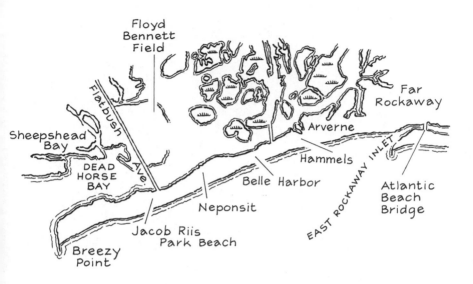

Floyd Bennett Field

Flatbush Ave.

Sheepshead Bay

DEAD HORSE BAY

Far Rockaway

Arverne

Hammels

Belle Harbor

Neponsit

EAST ROCKAWAY INLET

Atlantic Beach Bridge

Jacob Riis Park Beach

Breezy Point

ATLANTIC OCEAN

2 / *Up on the Rolling Sea*

The sea ain' got no back door.

—Caribbean saying via Paule Marshall

Peter Specter's Sure Cure for Seasickness: Relax under the nearest apple tree.

No matter how many years I logged on the waters with *Tradition,* every season began with "raising the sail in fear." E.B. White's phrase is apt; we were tempting the fates and exposing ourselves to nature. Owners of great power yachts, the ones that sleep six and eat twelve, want a sense, however illusory, that they are masters of the sea. Ocean-sailing yachts, in contrast, are built to cope with the power of the angry sea far offshore. Not *Tradition,* or other coasting workboats. They were built to handle short passages through the steep seas and gathering winds before ducking around a point of land into a cove or inlet. When the wind kicked up angry whitecaps and whipped heavy spray across her decks, we always headed *Tradition* for the nearest safe harbor and quiet channel.

Sailors of old boats have reason to be especially fearful of the sea's unmeasured power. I worried that *Tradition* might break up under the constant pounding of plunging through steep chop, or that she would not buck the strong tides of the inlets and estuaries. She needed to be taken on voyages with a careful eye on the weather and the tide charts. We didn't push her hard enough to discover her limits. When Susan and I sailed her through the waters of New York City, we moved with the tides and the winds, at least as far as that was possible.

Like it or not, the voyage from Long Beach to the entrance to the New York harbor requires a short ocean passage. From the inlet formed by the western end of Long Beach Island and the eastern end of the Rockaways, it's about ten miles to Breezy Point at the western end of the Rockaways. Then the course heads northward into the city's outer harbor. When sailing *Tradition,* we always timed our departures to catch the last three hours of an ebbing tide so the current would sweep us through the sometimes treacherous East Rockaway Inlet, known as Debbs Inlet by the locals. After about two or three hours in the ocean on a westward heading, we would pick up the beginnings of the flood tide that would push us toward the Narrows and up into the city.

As we sailed out into the ocean under an endless sky, Manhattan's towers were barely visible beyond a broad expanse of waves. Only the highest buildings peaked above a sliver of sand and a sea of green marsh. Away from the confines of my home channel, I always felt a rush of emotion that I connected with Irving Howe's description of "the American Newness." Howe was one of my mentors when I first came to the City University Graduate Center in 1973 where he was a professor, and his term evoked for me the excitement early observers felt when they described the teeming seas and skies of these New World shores. From the ocean, with the city so diminished, you can look afresh at the American shore and imagine what it was like in its pristine state. For Howe, the American Newness also referred to the Emersonian rejection of Old World traditions and constraints in favor of new understandings and experiences of life in the New World. But in the newness lay the heady temptation to reject all traditional values in favor of radical indivdualism and a leveling egalitarianism. Howe wrote that Americans who wish to conserve what is of lasting value "must veer and tack, stressing one moment the traditionalist and at another the populist option." Our era of conservative individualism was for Howe "a moment to invoke the tradition of fraternity and embrace Huck with Jim, Ishmael with Queequeg, opening once more upon democratic vistas." The folksinger Pete Seeger's restored sloop, the *Clearwater*, and the annual Clearwater Hudson River Festival are ambitious public efforts in the Hudson Valley at just this embrace of the democratic vistas. So, in a more personal fashion, were our harbor voyages on *Tradition*.

While I loved the adventure of being on the ocean and yet still at the city's edge, Susan suffered from rather severe seasickness and had little fondness for this part of the voyage. Fortunately, the ocean trip was short enough so that by the time she was becoming ill, we were usually just about to head into calmer waters.

On one trip, we planned to spend some time cruising in our favorite haunts in the lower harbor and especially in Jamaica Bay. A direct trip up to the entrance to Long Island Sound—from Long Beach to the Throgs Neck Bridge—took from twelve to fourteen hours of straight sailing and motoring. Ocean passage notwithstanding, the sailing was rather easy, but social plans and work obligations made it more complicated.

Before we could make way from Long Beach, we needed to leave a car at Jamaica Bay where we would end the first leg of our journey. My old friend Jules wanted to join us and welcomed a trip back through his native Brooklyn. He agreed to have me pick him up at Dead Horse Bay at the bottom of Flatbush Avenue so we could leave his car there for the return trip. Meanwhile, our friends Miriam and Gary would be joining us in Long Beach to complete the crew that day, and they would be driving from the North Shore of Long Island, carrying some of the victuals for the voyage.

I found Jules with no delay after a forty-minute drive through the Rockaways to Jamaica Bay. The trip reminded me of endless hours driving through that stretch of urban beach during the 1970s when I was working as a planner with the U.S. Department of Interior's National Park Service. My job was to assess the likely social impacts of federal environmental plans and to help organize public discussions about plans for Gateway National Recreation Area, which brought environmental restoration and new forms of urban recreation to much of the western end of the Rockaways. Back then, they were the lonely and depressed Rockaways. Long stretches of public housing were interspersed with decayed and burned-out old bungalows of the Irish Rockaways. With the economic boom of the nineties and the end of the crack epidemic, the neighborhoods I passed through on my drive to Brooklyn were in much better condition. There were still far too many unemployed young men on the corners, but less of the desperate furtiveness and fewer ominous gatherings by darkened storefronts. The auto trip that warm Sunday was easy and fast, and when Jules and I got to the boatyard in Long Beach, Miriam and Gary had arrived and were helping Susan stow gear and food. It was time to cast off.

We got a quick start through the open Long Island Railroad bridge. Some of our boatyard neighbors waved us off. They knew well that it was always something of a big deal to start the boating season by taking the old scow on a cruise into the city.

Reynolds Channel was filled with fishing boats and power cruisers of all description, and even a few sails, mainly moving away from the ocean. The breeze had come up strong, probably more than fifteen knots, with gusts up to twenty. Under full sail, *Tradition* couldn't hold course in wind that strong. With each heavy gust she tried to point her bow into the wind. It was a great struggle at the wheel to hold her on course against the "weather helm." We needed to shorten sail by reefing. A "reefed" sail has the same airfoil shape but presents less surface to the wind. After some adjustments we had a smooth curve of sail at the luff (the edge of sail along the mast). I turned *Tradition* downwind, her shortened sail billowed out, and she headed along the channel toward the ocean.

Tradition sailed with quiet, assured power, but her weather helm made steering difficult in the congested channel. As we slipped under the Atlantic Beach Bridge, I saw that we were heading too close to a motor yacht anchored in mid-channel. *Tradition*'s wheel was all the way over, but she headed directly for the yacht, which was crowded with fishing and lounging guests. I hurried to dump wind from the sail, and *Tradition* eased off the collision course. Just to be safe and gain more steering room, I quickly tried to fire up the engine. Just then a gust of wind pushed us dangerously close to the yacht. The colicky engine failed to catch. I watched helplessly, the rudder over as far as it could be pushed. *Tradition*'s port bilge caught the yacht's swim platform with a sickening crunch, and there were fierce shouts and curses from the yacht. I offered profuse apologies and blushed. The yacht owner had seen the event and graciously called out not to worry about it, perhaps knowing that he should not have anchored in the middle of a busy channel just under the bridge. At the yacht's stern another person pointed to say we had sustained damage to our hull. Still another glowered at us as if ready to board with a cutlass. But under sail and power we moved steadily out into the widening channel toward the ocean.

The damage was not grave. The collision had gouged a nasty two-foot scratch above the waterline, but it was mainly cosmetic and nothing that some sanding and paint couldn't fix. The tide and winds were moving us well out into the inlet, so we cut the engine. I sighed: a departure, but a lubberly one.

Debbs Inlet is well dredged and marked by buoys, but like all the major inlets along the Atlantic coast, it is often challenging. The ebbing tide that sped our way through the inlet was countered by the prevailing southwest wind. The action of wind against tide built up a steep chop, often confused further by huge cross seas churned by speeding power yachts. Port-bound fishing boats trailed crying flights of gulls and terns, eager to catch the scraps of fish being thrown from the stern by fisherman engaged in the tasks of filleting. A few times we were rolled in the cockpit and sprayed by slapping waves, but *Tradition* handled the confused inlet with little pounding and strain.

The ocean was rougher than I had expected. Four-foot swells were crested with occasional whitecaps. Fortunately the breeze was steady off our port quarter, and with her sail shortened *Tradition* churned along with reassuring power. Now and then the seas rolled her somewhat and the strong gusts pointed her out to sea. In the steady wind she eased toward shore, and I realized we would make a good course. But then we were forced to sail seaward again to avoid an immense dredging barge about a half-mile outside the inlet. We did some extra tacking in the seas, and *Tradition* moved through the wind and waves with aplomb. The stress of the inlet passage eased, and I began to calm down from the embarrassment of the collision. I felt the joy of the boat's easy motion over the seas. Each wave seemed to raise her a bit higher than the last. Apartment buildings that moments before had loomed on the shoreline quickly receded to a jagged horizon edge. Breakers along the shore become the distant city's ruffled sleeve. The metropolitan region dwindled against the visible curve of the earth and sea.

In the next few minutes *Tradition* was about two miles offshore and the broad Rockaway beaches narrowed to a ribbon. There were probably no fewer fishing boats to be seen here than in Reynolds Channel, but they were lost against the sweep of ocean waves. At the horizon, a line of freighters curved landward toward the Ambrose light, visible on its stilts at the ocean entrance to the city. Above the ships, jets bound for Kennedy airport traced a steady procession through the eastern skies.

We could barely make out the people who stood before the waves at the water's edge: here and there a group of children, adults flying kites or surf casting. I imagined catching a glimpse of wild Walt the beachcomber, his beard swinging like a wind vane, dogged by bounding street urchins. Whitman did a lot of declaiming to the gulls and sandpipers. The barrier islands were sparsely settled when he roamed "fish-shaped Paumanok's" silver beaches. Free from the city and "all that blab," he loved to loll on the sand to watch the clouds and waves roll past his body stretched along a curve of beach. Following his example, I sometimes shouted poetry from the deck of *Tradition*. My voice, lost in the wind, carried nowhere.

> Forests at the bottom of the sea, the branches and leaves,
> Sea-lettuce, vast lichens, strange flowers and seeds, the
> thick tangle, openings, and pink turf,

Different colors, pale gray and green, purple, white, and
    gold, the play of light through the water,
Dumb swimmers there among the rocks, coral, gluten,
    grass, rushes, and the aliment of the swimmers,
Sluggish existences grazing there suspended, or slowly
    crawling close to the bottom,
The sperm-whale at the surface blowing air and spray, or
    disporting with his flukes

My boyhood hero was a special kind of loafer in the frenzied commercial city. He was "Walt Whitman, an American, one of the roughs, a Kosmos, Disorderly fleshy and sensual . . . eating drinking and breeding." And he was the man who wrote, "Whoever degrades another degrades me," a good shipmate.

We were heading west along the beach, but the most favorable point of sail nudged us shoreward. On this brief ocean passage it's important to bear off the beach coast, so we tacked once away from our destination to gain distance from the lee shore. Nearer to the beach were shifting sandbars and shallow spots where the waves gathered in long shoals of dangerous breakers, especially on the approach to the western end of the Rockaways. We needed to head out in the direction of the Ambrose Channel to avoid the shallows. To the southwest, across the New York Bight, that vast triangle of land and ocean from Block Island to New Jersey's Cape May, the Jersey Highlands and the barest outline of Sandy Hook marked the beginning of the Jersey Shore. But we were still surging over the waves along the Rockaways, very much on the New York side of the Bight.

Tradition had an appealing, rhythmic way of nosing effortlessly over the swells. The regular creak of her rigging working against the wind and the rocking motions of the sea made me feel sleepy and secure. Our crew lolled on the comfortable cockpit benches. The catboat's faded red sail and her black gaff created a sharp tableau against the deep blue of the sky. Along the Rockaway shore, Harlem's A train rumbled along an elevated track that from the sea resembled a Roman aqueduct.

From *Tradition*'s ship-to-shore radio the tinny din of the city bounced off the sails, an invisible, supersonic wind of crackling pleas and throaty commands, a confusing chatter of "standing by, over" . . . "Comeback Lady Lu," "This is Delta 467, approaching on the R47"—the voices in the air of ground control and air pilot, stockbroker and real estate agent, party boat deckhands speaking in flounder code, moms anxious about dinner:

> "Where ya been? Johnny and Kerry been here fer hours, where ya been?"
> "We're out in the canyon, Ma, be home later, go ahead'n eat."
> "What canyon? You said you'd be home for dinner, jeez, and now it's all dried out. Thanks a lot."

Lately much of the blab from the continental shelf and the deep Hudson Canyon has been shunted into cellular silence. A partial calm reigns the airwaves, yet the marine operator is still there and the Coast Guard channels are often busy with hailings. And these are only the channels one hears most easily. They are the audible bands among far more channels, waves and waves of channeled talk blasting through the clouds and out to the sun, endless waves of thought and intelligible noise, the voices of the pundit chorus, the warnings and opinions, the citations and quotations. Closer inshore and up the harbor the city wind carries the whistles and horns, the clackety-clack of steel subway wheels, the thumping of construction trucks rolling over steel plates in the streets and the screeches of power-station cranes. On the streets you don't normally encounter the wind unless suddenly it whips around a corner building in an autumn or winter blast and forces you to lean against its force. But on the ocean the wind and the clouds rule, and the rush of the water fills the senses, fully and gratefully drowning the broadcast stream.

Every few minutes I marked our passage against the different neighborhoods that appeared along the shore. The high-rise buildings near Debbs Inlet were interspersed with older buildings and public housing for the elderly. Not visible from the ocean were the many yeshivas and shuls of Orthodox Jewish Far Rockaways, or the small churches of the African-Americans, that gave the neighborhood so much of its polyglot character.

Gradually, we came abeam of the Arverne neighborhood, where a sudden gap appeared in the façade of beachfront buildings. Dune grasses were reclaiming a vacant property where summer bungalows had been razed and never rebuilt. Why should such a prime beachfront area of four or five square blocks have remained unbuilt? How it became a slum reveals a more callous, mean-spirited, and wasteful side of the American Newness.

Half a century ago, agents of Robert Moses, New York's commissioner of public works, the city and state's master builder during much of the twentieth century, had relocated black and Puerto Rican families in the rickety Arverne summer bungalows after razing their existing neighborhoods inside the city. In his masterful biography of Moses, historian Robert Caro wrote that the bungalows at mid-century were "flimsy structures, each barely big enough to accommodate a single family." Earlier in the century they had been charming places for summer rental by Irish, Italian, and Jewish New Yorkers. In the interests of "slum clearance" and public-housing construction, however, the authorities declared them year-round dwellings and "temporarily" moved the displaced black and Puerto Rican families to shiver through the winter in them. Thousands of poor families were moved far from familiar jobs. And many Irish families mourned the loss of their summer community. The blacks and Puerto Ricans, who were finally relocated again to the high-rise public-housing apartments in the Arverne and Hammels neighborhoods of the Rockaways, had a difficult time making a go of life on the city's ocean edge. Builders who would normally drool at the prospect of plunking a nest of luxury condos on that vacant stretch of Rockaway Beach hesitated, mainly for fear of the "element" in the surrounding blocks. So the prime oceanfront property at Arverne was unintentionally allowed to revert to dune and beach grass.

OVER THE WAVES I could also just make out the dark shapes of rock jetties, each spaced about a city block apart, spanning the entire length of the Rockaways. Each beach was named after the nearest perpendicular street: Beach 149th Street, Beach 177th Street, and so on. People referred to this space between the jetties as "their beach." The jetties were also a reminder of the hotly contested political economy of sand.

Jetties help stabilize many of our East Coast barrier islands, or at least they give an illusion of stability that is periodically shattered by hurricanes in the summer and nor'easters in the winter. Big storms can cut inlets into the bays or wipe out entire beaches. Global warming and a rising ocean threaten to make the barrier islands even more precarious and more off-limits for construction. The rock jetties diminish the power of the longshore currents; they help prevent waves from scouring the sand during storms by slowing the flow of sand particles along the shore, forcing the sand to be deposited on the beaches. But the jetties also alter forever the beaches' appearance and impede their continual shaping and reshaping by the forces of wind and water. Once a community on a barrier island begins to stabilize its beaches with jetties, the currents eddying past the last jetty scour sand from the neighbors' unprotected beaches downstream. This phenomenon creates strong incentives for everyone along the barrier island to build jetties. Some environmentalists urge jetty removal and a return to the natural barrier island ecology, but the majority demand protection of their property and insist that eroded beaches or unwanted inlets be filled in with sand pumped at great public expense from offshore "borrow pits" by the Army Corps of Engineers. Eventually, the jetties hem in the barrier islands from inlet to inlet, as we see on the Rockaways and Long Beach Island, and so much of the Jersey Shore.

About two hours into our ocean passage, the blocks of apartment houses gave way to the single-family neighborhoods of Neponsit and Belle Harbor, largely upper-middle-class Jewish beach enclaves that end at Jacob Riis Park. Now part of Gateway National Recreation Area, Riis is another Robert Moses landmark along the lines of Jones Beach, which it preceded. At Riis Park, grass grows through the cement of an underutilized, 9,000-space parking lot; the park has minimal mass-transit access for the people of central Brooklyn, who often prefer the more crowded Coney Island, Brighton or Manhattan beaches which they can reach by subway.

At Riis Park we were sailing parallel to the shallow bar where the infamous *Golden Venture* went up on the Rockaway shore in 1993. There is no marker. Hundreds of ships have been wrecked along that innocent-looking stretch of beach; many of them, in the era before radar and global positioning systems, were thrown off course in storms or lost in dense fog as they vainly sought the passages among the sandbars into the lower harbor. But the *Golden Venture*'s grounding on these familiar sands was a connection to the legacy of piracy on our seas.

I glanced at our charts to check the water depths parallel to the beach where the *Golden Venture* hit a submerged sandbar. We were about a mile offshore, but I knew the freighter's deadly landfall was a mere two hundred yards off the western end of Riis Park beach where a bar extends a few hundred feet into the ocean and the breakers smash farther away from the beach. The chart showed the ocean depths under *Tradition* to be about thirty-five feet, but about a quarter-mile from the shore the depths were a mere fifteen feet and abruptly went to five feet at the sandbar. The rounded waves passing easily under *Tradition* quickly built up into breaking peaks that could easily hurl an errant ship onto the shallows.

The *Golden Venture* was a dismal freighter contracted by a crew of "snakeheads," professional smugglers in the United States and China who deal in human cargoes. They had packed the rusted tramp steamer with almost three hundred Chinese men, planning to slip them into the port where they would immediately become wage slaves in restaurants and garment sweatshops. The men suffered in the ship's filthy hold for almost a hundred days before smashing against the sandy coast.

The plan had been for smaller powerboats to meet the freighter somewhere off Sandy Hook and spirit the passengers into a coastal harbor in the night. After two such meetings failed to take place, the crew apparently mutinied and took control of the ship. At 2:00 A.M. on a dark, foggy night in early June, the

Golden Venture ran aground at Riis beach in a heavy sea. Hundreds of the men jumped into the cold ocean to chance the swim to shore. Most were wearing only their underwear and were carrying their few possessions in plastic bags. Many did not know how to swim, especially in the heavy surf. Their screams for help drew police and Coast Guard boats from all the nearby rescue stations. Most of the men were pulled from the surf, while others managed to swim ashore, where they shivered in the sand or wandered off in the hope of walking to freedom. Eight were drowned immediately; two died later in local hospitals. Peter Kwong, an expert on immigration to the city, wrote that the few who survived the Rockaway surf and escaped into the city were pursued by the snakeheads, to whom they owed substantial sums—more than $38,000 each. Most of the half-naked men were picked up by the police and spent long months in immigration prison, another form of official cruelty for the tempest-tossed victims of modern piracy.

The *Golden Venture*'s Indonesian captain, Amir Humuntal Lumban Toobing, pleaded guilty to conspiracy and smuggling but also claimed that the smugglers had taken control of the ship by force. After serving forty-one months of jail time in a federal prison, he was returned to Indonesia. But the lure of smuggling along the American coasts proved to be too strong. In 1997 he was caught with two Americans after sailing across the Pacific from Thailand in a fifty-four-foot sailboat carrying six tons of marijuana.

In the aftermath of the *Golden Venture* deaths, the Immigration and Naturalization Service also indicted attorney Robert Porges, head of a Manhattan firm that the INS claimed was fronting for the snakeheads. The federal authorities charged Porges and his firm with filing at least seven thousand false claims of asylum for aliens the snakeheads had smuggled into the country, for which Porges' fees totaled over $13 million. And this indictment merely exposed the beginnings of the network of snakeheads, their allies in Taiwan, China, and the United States, and the desperate families who are beholden to them. On a research trip to China's Wenshou and Fuzhou cities, original home to many of the smuggled, sociologist Peter Kwong spoke with the families of *Golden Venture* survivors and others whose adult children had been caught in similar bungled smuggling efforts. Since money mailed home from the United States was a primary source of income for many families in the province, most of these older parents were suffering from the failure of their children to successfully gain work in the sweatshops and kitchens of the promised land. One distraught parent told Kwong, "Once they make enough to send home, the elders can retire from the fields and the family can build houses and pay for daughters' weddings . . . [but instead] the head of the household, a great-grandfather who is nearly 80, had to harvest and thresh rice under the brutal July sun."

These are but new wrinkles on the old search for the American Dream, a quest that still often leads to piracy. There's fast money to be made smuggling cigarettes, booze, pot, purloined shellfish, gasoline, cocaine, wage slaves, you name it. The outer harbor offers plenty of places to sneak in from the ocean instead of going up into the port itself. In the marshy coves along Jamaica Bay, or Raritan Bay, or up the Navisink River on the Jersey side of the harbor, there are men with fast boats who make night dashes out to meet larger boats out in the ocean where illegal goods are transferred. I once knew a smuggler who doubled as a striped bass poacher. On particularly dark nights, when the fish were chasing smaller bait fish into the bays, he would use his motorboat to corral the big bass in the shallows of a creek where he could net them and fill boxes with the valuable fish, far beyond his legal limit.

When New York was a muddy frontier outpost, pirates and privateers picked their way over the many shoals and fog banks of these waters in all weather. All the old maps of the New York Bight and the great harbor show that before the massive dredging of the Ambrose Channel and the other ship entrances, it was a tricky passage across a maze of sandbars often made impassable by breaking waves. Back then there were no permanent buoys or other modern aids to navigation.

A memorable, but almost entirely forgotten, page of the city's pirate history is the story of the *Castel Del Rey,* one of the most ghastly shipwrecks in New York's waters during the city's commercial infancy.

The *Castel Del Rey* was a privateer commanded by a local captain and crew of Yankee and Dutch seamen. Privateers, unlike outlaw pirate ships, were chartered to engage in state-sanctioned brigandage against the ships of hostile nations. The *Castel Del*

Rey was scheduled to sail from the New York harbor during the summer of 1704 under her captain, Robert Troup, and with the backing of three investors who were well known among the port's merchant speculators. The ship had made some profitable privateering cruises in the previous two years, so much so that a dispute between the captain and the investors about how to divide the prospective booty delayed the *Castel Del Rey*'s 1704 summer sailing. Privateering was the most lucrative venture in New York's port at the time. Successful plundering of French and Spanish merchant sailing ships brought the first supply of luxury goods, especially perfumes and fancy jewelry, to the rough and muddy New World seaport. The dispute between Captain Troup and his backers dragged on through the fall while the crew and the local merchants grew impatient. Finally the backers and the captain agreed on terms, and the *Castel Del Rey*'s crew bade farewell to their loved ones in anticipation of booty and glory.

It was early December by the time the interminable haggling was finished and the ship made ready. Ice was forming at night on the city streets. A long cold snap had taken the city when the *Castel Del Rey*, with 107 aboard, raised her sails fearlessly and set off for the sunlit islands of the Caribbean. But on the tricky sand flats that ringed the coast south of the Narrows, the ship struck a bar that extended almost fully across the mouth of New York harbor. In full sight of land, with the day waning, the captain dispatched a boat to shore to seek help. Winds from the northeast increased to gale force, the weather turned bitter cold, and freezing rain became an ice storm. As the waves ground her bottom against the bar, hull planks of the *Castel Del Rey* sprung under the pressure. Water rose in her hold until it filled the ship's cabins. Fierce wind gusts snapped in the ice-coated rigging. Sometime in the night, with the decks awash in heavy seas, the crew climbed onto the masts and yardarms to escape the rising water. Morning found the sailors and officers frozen like so many dead bats in the stiffened shrouds. Only five or six were alive, and barely. It was the worst sea disaster in the young port's history, made doubly tragic by its proximity to the safe harbors at nearby Sandy Hook and Great Kills, not far below the Narrows.

There is no marker for the crew of the *Castel Del Rey*, as there is none for the *Golden Venture*. The waters are the grave and monument. There were so many wrecks and disasters along the Long Island beaches during the age of sail and the first decades of the age of steam that only the most disastrous claim even a few lines in our city's collective memory. We set commemorative plaques for the victims of plane wrecks like those from TWA flight 800, which crashed on these shores forty miles or so to the east in the summer of 1996, but we have no way to fully understand these tragedies or celebrate their lost heroes. In our anxious haste to get where we're going, we would rather forget that transit disasters occur at all.

TRADITION PASSED THE *Golden Venture*'s grounding spot and moved into the currents around Breezy Point, on a course that would take us well seaward of the long jetty marking the western limit of the Rockaways. A rolling sea off our stern quarter made some of the crew seasick and all of us a bit queasy. Miriam heaved discreetly a few times while playing Scrabble with Susan, who was herself turning a pale shade of green. Jules was queasy but game as always. Gary and I were not much bothered. Before long we were rounding the long ocean jetty at Breezy Point, at the eastern edge of the great harbor, where a mournful horn warned all ships away from the rocks and reminded me again of shipwrecks and drownings.

I pointed out the wide and gleaming beach at the tip of Breezy Point. Acres of sand had gathered along the long jetty that we were beginning to round, adding scores of new acres to the wide beach. Before the environmental legislation of the seventies, this sand would have become another subdivision for beach homes, but it is now one of the East Coast's prime nesting areas for piping plovers. Known for their soft, organ-like call, the plovers are an endangered species that will nest and lay eggs in ruts only on a broad, warm beach. At Breezy Point they are carefully protected by watchful birders and National Park Service rangers. Their chief predators, which used to be raccoons and foxes, are now house cats. When the birds are no longer nesting, fisherman cast for bass and bluefish off the beach and jetty day and night.

A charge of adrenaline hit me just after we rounded Breezy Point: the wedges securing *Tradition*'s mast had come loose, and the mast was swaying against its stays instead of remaining solid in its place. A fierce tide rip drew us too far across the channel toward a shallow spot where the waves break. The breeze had freshened again, and with the helm all the way against its stops, we were plunging directly for the shallows and breakers. Most of my crew were either distracted by their seasickness or engrossed in watching flights of terns and gulls that dove in a feeding frenzy nearer to the Breezy Point shore, but Gary immediately saw our predicament. Fortunately, as the breeze slackened, *Tradition* resumed a safer course. I had no time to feel relieved. Almost immediately a strong gust blew us once again closer to the breaking seas. I could see the waves curling over into dangerous surf. They roiled a tormented green and white foam near the buoy marking the edge of the channel. Her wheel full over, *Tradition* was making a dash for those breakers. Gary didn't need to urge me to start the engine; my hand was already turning the ignition switch. The old Atomic Four kicked in with a bit of coaxing from the choke, and we soon had enough power to motor-sail into mid-channel, away from the tide rip. Out of danger and with plenty of helm for steering, I shut the engine again so we heard only the sounds of sea and air. Gary took the wheel while I went forward and did a quick, temporary tightening of the mast wedges.

The channel into Jamaica Bay began to curve eastward along the Rockaways. We were in calm water on the bay side of the barrier island peninsula, abeam of the gated Cooperative Community of Breezy Point, still famous in the city as a remnant of the Rockaways' "Irish Riviera." Houses in this beach village sell by word of mouth or are passed along from generation to generation. Students of the city's communities consider it the whitest enclave in an increasingly multiracial metropolis.

Far over the waves breaking on the Brooklyn shores to our north, we could make out the Coney Island boardwalk, the abandoned tower of the Steeplechase parachute ride, the swinging cars of the still-turning Wonder Wheel, and the Aquarium. Susan reminded me of the day in the sixties when we had come with thousands of other New Yorkers to mourn the final closing of Steeplechase, "the Happy Place." Woody Allen and Mel Brooks sat at a table trading quips and reminiscences with the public about the defunct amusement park and the attractions of a bygone era. But now a new minor-league baseball stadium hosts new generations of Coney Island visitors.

Closer to shore on our right, at the eastern edge of the Breezy Point community, there was another vacant stretch of Rockaway Beach, adjacent to a garish beach club. This isolated patch of dune and swale marked the spot where two unfinished high-rise apartment towers were blown into oblivion in the early 1980s, marking a new turn toward environmental restoration in the outer harbor. Almost twenty years earlier, in the late sixties, the windblown cement hulks had became a symbol among environmental activists in the Rockaways and elsewhere in the city of everything that was wrong with publically subsidized high-rise construction on the unstable barrier beaches. The crusade to raze them helped the Regional Plan Association build a broader citizens' movement, which culminated in 1972 when Congress passed the legislation to create Gateway and its sister park, the Golden Gate National Recreation Area in San Francisco Bay.

At the mouth of the New York harbor, Gateway unifies a bewildering array of natural areas and beach parks. The National Park Service at Gateway manages Robert Moses–era beaches like Jacob Riis Park, old military installations and shore batteries, all of New Jersey's Sandy Hook, the beaches of Staten Island's south shore, and most of the islands and shoreline of Jamaica Bay, including Floyd Bennett Field, a former military airfield and one of the early centers of flight in the nation. Almost thirty years after its creation, however, most New Yorkers would not be able to explain what, or exactly where, Gateway is. Unlike Jones Beach with its famous campanile and immense outdoor swimming pool, or Coney Island with its tottering amusement parks and easy access by subway, Gateway has no outstanding physical feature or easy transit access to make it stand out for millions of New Yorkers. The stretch of beach swale where the infamous high-rise skeletons were razed is only a monument to those who know its significance.

Gateway is a new species of national park, wrested from the real estate market and the military, devoted to understanding and protecting wetlands and marshes, piping plovers and horseshoe crabs, and a thousand other estuarine species. An unconventional national park, lacking a "crown jewel" natural feature, or a genuine battlefield, or bears or bison, Gateway is devoted to unheroic species and seemingly modest goals like sustainable recreation and environmental education. I'm sure biologist René Dubos, one of its early advocates, or the pioneering ecologist Aldo Leopold, would be proud of it. In the *Sand County Almanac* Leopold criticized the national parks as inadequate islands of preservation in a nation whose people lacked a "land ethic." He urged that we go beyond preservation of the continent's outstanding features, its yawning chasms and glaciered peaks, that we enhance the natural environment in our backyards and farms, and extend the land ethic inside the cities as well as in the wildlands.

We sailed *Tradition* on a comfortable broad reach along the Breezy Point Channel, past buoys pointing the way into Sheepshead Bay and on to Dead Horse Bay at the foot of Flatbush Avenue. Earlier that morning I'd reserved a guest slip in the Barren Island Marina. The marina is in Dead Horse Bay, a cove where an abattoir and glue factory once stood. Barren Island is also where Floyd Bennett Field is located. The island's name is a reminder that all tidal marshlands, like those in Jamaica Bay, were once regarded as barren and useless, fit mainly for the tons of garbage and cellar dirt used to fill them into solid real estate. Across Flatbush Avenue from the marina is Floyd Bennett, with vintage airplane hangars and runways of a historic airfield. The field is the largest single piece of open land in the city and hosts a forest upland, a huge expanse of community gardens, an environmental education center, and helicopter bases for the police and Coast Guard.

Our legs felt a bit wobbly when we walked on the dock and we all had tints of windblown color on our faces. We had made an ocean passage, however short, in a relic of American nautical history. Aside from a few anxious moments, it had been a splendid passage.

There was plenty of straightening up to do on *Tradition*. Her mast wedges needed looking after, and the engine's carburetor was suspect. The pump sopped up a slow leak with about thirty seconds of work every hour, but even this light pumping required a reliable battery system. I am not a compulsive boatkeeper, and except for the very basic straightening up on deck, *Tradition*'s needs could wait for tomorrow.

We piled into the car for the half-hour drive back to Long Beach, where we could celebrate our ocean exploits. *Tradition* was secure in the marina at Dead Horse Bay, Gateway National Recreation Area. Later in the week, to avoid dockage costs, Noah and I would move her to the fine anchorage just next to the marina, where she could stay until we resumed our voyages into Jamaica Bay.

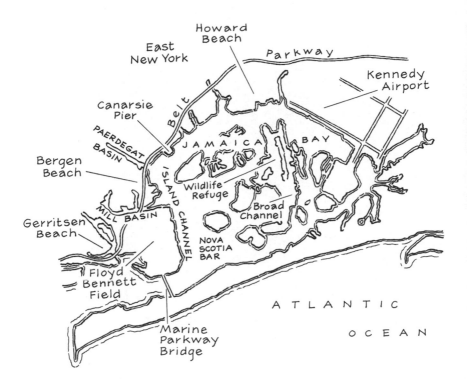

3 / *Jamaica Bay, Gateway*

> My cells are no longer the pure line entities I was raised
> with; they are ecosystems more complex than Jamaica Bay.
>
> —Lewis Thomas, *Lives of a Cell*

*S*ome days after our landing at Dead Horse Bay, we sailed from the marina and headed east for the interior of Jamaica Bay. It was a glowing workday morning in May, the type that comes with a spring fever advisory. On board were Susan and our daughter Johanna, home for a brief respite from her lab; Professor John Mollenkopf, my City University friend and ardent student of everything about Brooklyn; and Daisy and Bosun, our salty dogs.

With two reefs in the sail against a whistling breeze from the northwest, we scudded on a favorable tide under the Gil Hodges Memorial Bridge. This is the double-tower span named for the Dodger hero, the bridge that carries Flatbush Avenue over the water and out to the Rockaways at Jacob Riis Beach. Once clear of the bridge and sailing along the edge of Floyd Bennett Field, we would enter the bay itself.

At first we had some difficulty clearing the bridge span. Crosscurrents and tide rips made sailing a momentary adventure. After two tries and a bit of body English, we came out into the Island Channel, east of the bridge, on a starboard tack. Gusts of spring wind billowed the shortened sail. *Tradition* carved an impressive bow wave that gurgled and sang as we made through the chop. To our left was Barren Island and the airfield, now Gateway headquarters. To our right, looking due south across the channel, the Rockaways extended barrier-island thin along the ocean shore. The marshlands were sorely pressed on the Rockaway bay shore, where walls of concrete and pilings were interspersed with commercial development, roadways, the occasional marina, a major bridge crossing at Broad Channel and the large Marine Sciences High School. In the distance along the ocean shore rose the phalanx of public-housing apartments called Hammels. And along it all ran the elevated tracks of the A train, which turn north beyond Broad Channel to cross Jamaica Bay and wind through Brooklyn and the boroughs beyond.

We headed away from the Rockaway shores in the direction of a low, grassy island outside the main channel. This was the hummock known as Nova Scotia bar, and without a slight course change we would be heading toward its hidden mudflats at the channel's edge. Water depths in Island Channel are a reassuring twenty-five feet at low tide, but just east of the channel's buoy markers, where we were heading, the depths went immediately to two feet, one foot, half a foot. It was easy to run aground on the channel's edges, even in a catboat, and especially in one with a steel keel that likes to stick in any mud above four feet of depth.

Island Channel and the other main Jamaica Bay reaches, however, offered spectacular sailing for the catboat. We had rounded the southeastern corner of Floyd Bennett and needed to get the wind on the other side of the sail. We executed a smart controlled jibe where the boom swung across the deck and caught the wind on the desired tack, without having to tack in a full circle. The simple but well-handled maneuver impressed my friend John, who was more accustomed to sailing on racing sloops than pottering in creaky old workboats. From the middle of Jamaica Bay, the towers of Manhattan appeared a distant toy city above an illusory sea of light green marsh grasses. In the midground, the channel led toward the arching parkway bridges and the walled canals beyond.

Neighborhoods under the Belt Parkway bridges and up into the Brooklyn marshes are fantastic, ur–New York tidal basin villages. Picturesque, sometimes gaudy homes line the canals built on the filled marsh of Mill Basin, Paerdegat Basin, Bergen Beach, Howard Beach, and the other creeks feeding into the bay.

Until quite recently, Jamaica Bay's very existence as a living tidal estuary was in serious doubt. The story of its preservation and restoration demands to be told and retold as often as possible, which is probably why the late Dr. Lewis Thomas, essayist and former chancellor of Sloan-Kettering, alludes to it in *Lives of a Cell,* when he compares a living cell with Jamaica Bay. His cells and Jamaica Bay are indeed miraculous ecosystems. They are subject to biological laws and to the more chaotic influences of an ever-changing external environment. But Jamaica Bay is also a sociological environment of the first order of complexity. I doubt more is known about places like Jamaica Bay than about the living cell and its enzymes and molecular transfers.

For thousands of centuries before human habitation, the bay's evolution answered to purely geological and biological forces. At least in theory, these forces and their effects are largely understood by our natural sciences. But a few thousand years ago, hardly a blip in geological time, humans began living around the bay and began influencing its evolution. The Canarsee Indians, a band of the great Algonquin people, favored some species of shellfish and plants and discouraged others. Their middens of shells and other leavings created the first landfills, but these were minor intrusions compared to what would come later. With Dutch settlement in the 1600s came more efforts to control and exploit the bay. Its flowing creeks turned the wheels of their tide mills. Salt-hay farming flourished on the waving thick spartina grasslands, and camps were established where shooters could prey on the flights of waterfowl. During the next three hundred years the bay, like most others along the continent's grassy skirt of marshes and sea channels, became a source of almost inexhaustibly rich harvests. The aboriginal people were quickly and sometimes violently pushed away to the ever-expanding edges of European settlement. Some hardy folk began building small villages of shacks along the bay's soft edges and on some of the larger hummocks in its interior. These were fishermen and baymen, the "swamp Yankees" who sought escape from the city and were the ancestors of people in the existing marsh villages of Jamaica Bay, like Broad Channel, Hamilton Beach, and others well hidden from the roads.

During the second half of the nineteenth century and accelerating well into the next, there was a new invasion of the bay. In the industrial age, no task of earthmoving or swamp filling seemed beyond a machine's power. Boosters, speculators and developers eagerly began exploiting the bay as nascent real estate. Their promotions touted it as a promising zone for construction of seaside resorts. Fancy racetracks, opulently rustic fantasy hotels, ferry docks, and yacht clubs all began appearing here and there along the bay. The first great urban projects were pleasure destinations for the city's rich and hopeful. Then more mass residential summer colonies were thrown up, and eventually airports and other industrial sites. Grassy hummocks around Barren Island were filled and layered with garbage and construction fill materials, joined into larger islands for huge expanses of concrete and macadam runways. The bay became part of a new order of urban estuaries. It seemed far from the city and unencumbered by existing dense settlements, so it was fair territory for the fillers and builders of the Industrial Age.

By the 1950s the bay was alive with activity, and its remaining wetlands were seen as an urban wilderness, almost outside the law, and a good dumping ground for murdered gangsters and the hulks of stolen cars. It was not certain that there would be a future for anything recognizable as Jamaica Bay, just as today it is difficult to recognize the abused remnants of a natural estuarine environment in the oiled wetlands of Flushing Meadow, Newtown Creek dividing Brooklyn from Queens, or between the parking lots on the New Jersey Meadowlands or in the Bronx's Pelham Bay wetlands.

WITH THESE THOUGHTS very much on my mind, I proposed to the crew that we turn east and sail deeper into the grassy hummocks and hidden islands of the bay's interior. My proposal was greeted with much skepticism. Susan and Johanna wanted to sail in the broad reaches to avoid running aground in the buggy marshes. My friend John, an inveterate explorer of Brooklyn's neighborhoods, wanted to get a glimpse of Mill Basin from the water, which would require sailing under the eponymous bridge, clearance thirty feet at high tide.

The bright sunlight, *Tradition*'s easy motion over the chop and the simple thrill of being out on the bay made me a particularly feckless captain. I just wanted to keep sailing. I *did* hope that after a detour into urban Mill Basin we might make it to Canarsie Pier, into the bay's marshy interior.

We were debating the pros and cons of our course and reaching a friendly consensus when a sturdy New York City Ports and Terminals workboat came charging up on our stern. Its twin diesels churned a massive wake that *Tradition* surfed with ease. Three young and stalwart deckhands waved and gave us high signs as their vessel made its way toward the Belt Parkway bridge leading into Mill Basin. That settled the matter.

"Let's follow those cute guys and see what they're doing up in the basin," Johanna ordered with Susan's support.

For the next fifteen minutes we followed the workboat and its hunks past the eastern edge of Floyd Bennett Field, along Island Channel. We were on a beam reach, *Tradition*'s most powerful point of sail, and since the workboat was moving at about seven knots and we were doing almost six, we managed to stay reasonably close to it. We sailed past the Coast Guard helicopter base and a broad section of runway that dropped into the bay itself for seaplane launching, an ideal spot for launching small sailing vessels. Before budget cuts, the Park Service had run an immensely popular school sailing program at the ramp. Students from local schools could sign up for lessons in the marine arts and have a chance to sail small fiberglass boats under professional instruction. That program went the way of night basketball and other so-called excesses of public spending.

Beyond the wide runways of this section of Floyd Bennett, we reached a corner of what is now called the field's "north forty." Pines and scrub forest have claimed these rare acres at the outer limits of the old runways. The "north forty" has become home to upland birds of all kinds, including an array of hawks. It is a perfect habitat for pheasants and grouse and small mammals, including raccoons and possum, and even some foxes who wisely travel only at night.

We hauled in the sheet and pointed upwind to turn the corner at the edge of Floyd Bennett, where it heads northward. Shortly afterward the channel ducked below the bridge and into Mill Basin. The workboat had slowed at the bridge, probably on a mission to check the depth of channels and position of local aids to navigation. We passed it again as we slipped just under the bridge, while the young deckhands watched to see whether the mast would clear the span. We were under engine and sail power to make sure we'd have plenty of rudder to maneuver through the bridge's narrow channel.

Mill Basin's backyards end at private docks that host watercraft of all kinds. Houses sit close to each other, and the place has the strong feel of a New York Italian-American fantasy: Venice in postwar Brooklyn, a bulkheaded waterland paradise.

Houses on both sides of the narrow channel muffled any wind gusts. For the first time that day we felt the sun's heat; the engine's steady putter echoed off the garages. Even with slackened sail, *Tradition* and her crew of outsiders must have been a strange sight through the picture windows in the houses that lined our passage. But it was a working morning and we spied not one Mill Basin indigene, although we saw much evidence of serious vegetable gardening. Annuals set in pots of every description bloomed everywhere, grapevines wound over trellises, and elaborate barbecue areas spoke of happy family gatherings to come later in the spring and summer. After a few minutes of backyard voyeurism, sweat rising quickly in the full sun and windless air, it was easy for me to convince the crew to scoot back under the bridge to catch the cool strong breeze on a sail in the channel beyond Barren Island and east to far Canarsie.

We sailed for about thirty minutes on a blustery broad reach, tacking up to the bridge over the Belt at the Paerdegat Basin where there was clearance for *Tradition*'s short mast, but we had no time for full exploration. Instead, we tacked across the channel for the fun of it and tied up at Canarsie Pier, one of the many wonderful surprises on a cruise in Jamaica Bay.

Canarsie is the name New Yorkers often invoke when they want to indicate a distant place they would have no reason to visit ("It's somewhere far, like Canarsie or something . . ."). Before federal park officials became involved in managing the bay, Canarsie Pier—at the very top of Jamaica Bay just off the Belt Parkway but at the very bottom of vast Brooklyn—was run down like many other forgotten city piers or parks. There was a ramshackle hot dog stand and general-purpose short-order joint leaning against the pier's cement piles. For years Frank Abbracciamento, whose stand it was, worked patiently with the Park Service to get the pier renovated, with a place on it for his stand. When we arrived, Canarsie Pier had been rebuilt as a grand and delightful shoreline park, with shade trees along its length and ample room for fishing and relaxing. There was space to park the car and simply look out across the breezy reaches of the wide bay to the majestic jetliners descending for their landings at JFK International. Alongside the pier stood the new and spacious Abbracciamento's Restaurant, with an inviting dock. We tied *Tradition* there while we stretched our legs, walked the dogs, and ordered some sandwiches and drinks to take from the restaurant. Above us, along the edge of the pier itself, stood clusters of regulars, fishermen with extensive tackle and a single-minded attention to their tasks. Among them strolled couples and family groups. The children eagerly questioned the fishermen about their catch and shrieked with delight at the sight of fish brought out proudly from big plastic buckets.

When we weren't people-watching from *Tradition's* deck, we relaxed in the sun and stared out into the reaches of Jamaica Bay. All those green patches in the bay had names: Nova Scotia Bar, Ruffle Bar, the Raunt, Canarsie Pol, Hamilton Beach, Rulers Bar Hassock, Negro Bar, Barbados Bar, Blackwall Marsh . . . places likely unknown to the millions who drove a mile a minute across lower Queens and Brooklyn along the Belt.

Looking out at the water and waving spartina grass, it's easy to forget that Canarsie Pier was built early in the 1900s as a beachhead of the proposed industrial superport that would relieve the intense congestion of the Brooklyn and Manhattan docks on the East River. Mercifully, that industrial development never materialized. Instead one can look southward over the bay, away from the cars and the horizon of Brooklyn apartments, to imagine what this part of the world was like when the Canarsie Indians and Dutch settlers coexisted on the bay for a couple of generations: settlements in a wilderness of spartina grass that seemed to grow there for them alone to harvest as salt hay and to pasture domestic animals, amid creeks and channels still lush with wildfowl, fish, clams, and oysters.

Upland, on the Belt Parkway, the traffic slowed to a crawl for no apparent reason. But this was mild compared to the endless creeping traffic jams on hot beach days in July or August. In a few moments we would be under way again to retrace our course back to Dead Horse Bay, but the urge to lose myself in the bay's interior would not go away. I resolved to make it my business to escape somehow on the boat into the nearby "wilderness" of the islands and marshes.

A FEW DAYS LATER, I sailed again for some solitary exploration. I rarely went exploring alone in the city, but this solo voyage into Jamaica Bay was a special adventure in urban cruising.

I went for three days of solitude, without dogs, children, friends, or spouse. Early in the morning I guided *Tradition* on a flooding tide once again under the Gil Hodges Memorial (a.k.a. Marine Parkway) Bridge. On the way into the bay's interior, I stopped to do some fishing along the edges of the channels. In almost no time I landed two porgies and then (after some annoying oaths to and from a croaking sea robin), I caught a nice summer flounder, a fluke, a keeper.

On a glorious run downwind, with *Tradition*'s boom payed out almost perpendicular to the beam, I sailed for hours on a light southwest wind through different channels and creeks and ended my sail in the North Channel, beyond Canarsie and into the green corridors of Pumpkin Patch Channel. When the channel narrowed, I rounded upwind to slow down and soon came in sight of the west pond of the Jamaica Bay Wildlife Refuge. *Tradition* swayed at anchor in one of the many quiet and somewhat hidden pools in the lush marsh while I lolled on deck and wrote an entry in her logbook. The spot I chose afforded a good binocular view of bird activity on the pond, but hid the boat from direct view of the Broad Channel village and the traffic on Cross Bay Boulevard. This anchorage was only a few hundred yards from the nearest convenience store and about half a mile from the subway stop on Broad Channel Island. Surrounded by the marshes and the narrow creeks that fed into Pumpkin Patch Channel, it seemed that the boat and I were alone on a sea of marsh grass under an infinitely curving bowl of fair sky. It was still May. The breeze carried the chill air of a colder ocean.

Later, I prepared the fish for dinner, along with some small red potatoes, all of which grilled quickly on the boat's outdoor charcoal cooker. To go with the crispy fish and roasted potatoes I had a tomato and red onion salad, some French bread, a ripe cheese, and a chilled Tavel, *Tradition*'s cabin house wine. Time spent in the wilderness among the creatures, I reasoned, merited some of the creature comforts.

After dinner, and a half-hour before sunset, I went exploring in the inflatable dinghy in narrow Horse Channel between Stony Marsh and Yellow Bar. I was hoping for a chance meeting with some shorebirds, but I had no immediate luck. My eyes were not yet accustomed to the marsh. So I rowed for a while away from

Tradition, her anchor light already swinging aloft, and away from the Wildlife Refuge, farther into the marsh toward the setting sun. And sure enough, as I was drifting, I noticed a rustle in the marsh grass. A clapper rail on stealthy feet was stalking evening mud bugs. Like most of the rails, close cousins to the ducks, the clapper rail is most handsome, with a long and straight beak set perfectly below a head that sweeps imperceptibly into a gracefully curving neck and then down into strong shoulders. Much loved by birders and hunters, the rails hunt fiddler crabs along the sandy edges of the marsh and in the looming darkness of the salt streams up in the grasses. Find the fiddlers and there you'll find a rail—but not clapping, just intently and quietly hunting. With their outsize claws waving in the current, the swift fiddler crabs ingest globs of debris shed from the ever-nourishing spartina grass. They fatten themselves to the rails' delight.

There was another brief flutter of wings above my head, and I looked up in time to get a long view of a soaring pair of glossy ibis. They are delicate gliders with jet-black bodies and rapier-curved beaks. Along with the osprey and peregrine falcons, they were almost erased from the bay earlier in the century, their dying eggs made paper-thin from the DDT mosquito sprays. Now, under the watchful eyes of birders and the federal rangers, who won't permit indiscriminate spraying, they are flourishing again and are among the bay's most cherished birds. Here in Jamaica Bay a *pax environmentalis* of federal protection spreads even to the insects that these birds must feed on.

I drifted, watching. There were waterfowl and other animals in every direction. I saw cormorants, terns, peeps, mallards, ruddies. Up another shadowy bend stood two snowy egrets, with their outrageous yellow boots and platinum punk haircuts. How chic, these mudbank sushi bars. The egrets were spearing for sand bugs, moving along the edge of the marsh with the herky giant steps of students at a party stepping over empty beer cans. Above my head a fluttering bat inscribed wide circles. The dinghy drifted, with just an occasional pull on an oar, toward the light fading over the distant toy city and the towers of the Verrazano-Narrows Bridge.

I turned to row back to *Tradition,* into the darkness. The last glimmers of light played on the grasses swaying in a breeze just strong enough to disperse the gnats and mosquitoes. Here and there I could see a quick flash of light glinting off the eye of a water rat or raccoon working the marshes up in the creeks, with lunch pails to fill. Beyond the creeks and marshes and over a darkening patch of rippling water I could see *Tradition*'s anchor light beckoning me home.

Back on board and sprawled on her wide cabin deck, I treated myself to a drink in honor of the end of the day. Night was falling quickly. There was no silence along with the gathering darkness. But here there was night, deep darkness, real night without streetlamps and security lights and billboards. The night allowed a rather nice display of evening stars even though I was well within the red glow of the city. From all directions came the sounds of the salt marsh, the *plop-swish* of birds landing, the flutter of wings and the occasional honk of a goose, and while there was also no relief from the distant mechanical screeches and honks of the city, these sounds blended in with those of the bay.

Sprawled flat out on *Tradition*'s cabin deck, taking in the illuminated complexity of the megalopolis from a dark point in the marsh on Jamaica Bay, I was reminded that a far different version of this view is the first glimpse of the United States for many of the city's contemporary immigrants and a large share of the nation's foreign tourists. The tired traveler jets down into Jamaica Bay for a night landing at JFK through a rush of confusing lights and green patches and water, a surreal vision of a subway advancing across a mudflat and a road bisecting a shadowy marsh, before traversing a desert of oily pavement and more confusing lights. But here in the bay, the airport was distant. The bay was immense yet comprehensible. The jets were landing into the prevailing southwesterly, which meant they came in over Nassau County on the other side of the airport rather than directly overhead. In one direction was the subway to the Rockaways, the lights of the village of Broad Channel, and beyond them the JFK runway lights. In another direction was the expanse of water and marsh where every so often flashing eyes pierced the grasses. I had rarely felt so alone and so small.

The wavelets slapping in friendly rhythm on the hull had an extremely calming effect. So did the wide expanse of the cabin and the low roof. I hurried to finish a log entry, for drowsiness was gaining on me. On *Tradition*'s overstocked library shelf just above my head were the works that saved Jamaica Bay: the Teals on the life and death of a salt marsh, the indispensable Roger Tory Peterson on birds, René Dubos, Rachel Carson, John Kieran, Elizabeth Barlow Rogers, and in a more fanciful category of reading there was Kenneth Grahame, Lewis Carroll's Snark ("who needs mercators, North Poles and equators, they are only conventional signs"), Edward Lear, and so many others. It always gave me agita to have to take up just one, and as always, I'd brought too many books. *Tradition*'s double berth and down sleeping bag were impossibly comfortable.

Just before I fell asleep that night, I was browsing through Joseph Mitchell's essays on the harbor, revisiting his friend Mr. "Happy" Zimmer, a displaced oyster dredger, who by mid-century had become a conservation officer in the lower harbor and Jamaica Bay. His job was to patrol the polluted and off-limits shellfish beds to make sure no one was taking clams or oysters illegally. Zimmer was a man who could bring his skiff into the Jamaica Bay marshes and sit up the entire night, never bored, engrossed in the stars and sounds of the bay, watchful for the arrival of the shellfish poachers.

One morning Mr. Zimmer becomes depressed. The marshes are doomed. The city has begun to dump garbage on them. It has already filled in hundreds of acres with garbage. Eventually, it will fill in the whole area, and then the Department of Parks will undoubtedly build some proper parks out there, and put in some concrete highways and scatter some concrete benches about.

I remember driving with my mother and father and baby brother Peter through Queens and Brooklyn, creeping our way in a late summer heat wave toward Flatland Avenue for a visit to Hanana, my grandmother. It was late in the summer of 1949 and the Brooks were playing the Phillies for the National League pennant. Jackie Robinson was making sensational plays at second and on the base paths. My father had been a hot shortstop in the cutthroat Manhattan Beach and Marine Park semipro leagues in the late twenties. He'd been recruited to join the Dodgers farm system but chose a life of labor law and city politics and remained a fanatic Dodger fan. We were all yelling into the car radio.

My father had taken the old Interboro (now proudly renamed the Jackie Robinson Parkway) from quaint Forest Hills in Queens to Brooklyn's East New York, down hot and congested Pennsylvania Avenue at the end of which, on the shore of Jamaica Bay, was a large and smelly garbage fill. At mid-century there were still many local breweries and small factories all over lower Brooklyn, some of which ran effluent into the marshes.

We were going to pick up Grandma and then go to Coney Island, the greatest, the ultimate. (How many times would I hear that it was too bad I would never know Feltman's where the hot dog was invented, or Luna Park? But glory of glories, there was still one vintage amusement park, George C. Tilyou's Steeplechase.) The steaming car crawled down Pennsylvania Avenue before emerging on the Belt Parkway, where there was an expanse of open water and cooler breezes and a sea of green marsh. The bay opened up, wetlands on either side of the six-lane parkway.

"Billy," my father said, "do you see all those small houses out in the bay?"

By day the bay shacks looked inviting, like so many rickety tree houses, and by night they shone with scores of twinkling lights and the promise of warm dinners, far off in the vast darkness beyond the highway.

"Moses wants to tear down all those bay houses," my father said. He explained that there were families out there who had them for generations. Moses had control over all these waters and wetlands and wanted to put up public housing on the Rockaways. But how, my father wondered, would the people he moved there ever find work?

I did not understand many of the things my father tried to explain to me then, but this Moses, I thought to myself, he seems powerful and easy to anger, like the biblical one. My father admired and hated (and probably envied) Robert Moses. He loved the master builder's achievements at Jones Beach and the parkways, but like many other New Yorkers, even before the ruthless bisecting of so many communities for the system of vehicle expressways, he disliked Moses' imperious and dictatorial personality. As a city labor commissioner, he'd had dealings with the far more fearsome, powerful commissioner of the Triborough

Bridge and Tunnel Authority, of parks, housing, and much else. My father had won a small victory in some contract negotiations and Moses had put him on his enemies list. My dad was proud of that.

Robert Moses deserves credit for establishing the Jamaica Bay Wildlife Refuge, close by my anchorage that night, the only wildlife preserve in the United States (in the entire world perhaps) accessible by subway. But Moses the Master Builder did not create the actual refuge as we know it on Ruler's Bar Hassock near Pumpkin Patch Channel. That was the work of a far different kind of New Yorker.

Much of the credit for the success of the Wildlife Refuge must go to a park horticulturalist and wildlife lover named Herb Johnson. He built the refuge and inspired others to follow his lead in preserving and restoring more of the natural areas in and around Jamaica Bay and the lower bay. When he arrived along the bay's grassy shores in 1951, there was no fresh water to invite waterfowl to stay and rest during their long migrations. Herb Johnson's assignment from Moses was to build a refuge, but no one told him how it was to be done. Johnson was the son of an estate gardener and knew how to create "the unkempt beauty of a seaside landscape," as landscape historian Elizabeth Barlow Rogers puts it.

I met Mr. Johnson at a number of Gateway planning meetings where he advised the federal authorities about continuing his work in Jamaica Bay. He was gray-haired and retired by then, an extremely modest man but a revered figure among the region's birders. He spoke with a rather heavy New York accent, and I most remember his animated descriptions of how Jamaica Bay was located at the confluence of two major branches of the continental bird migration: the Atlantic flyway extending down from the Maritimes of Canada and another from the shores of the Great Lakes. Water for the birds to land on and drink would be part of the secret to a successful refuge in Jamaica Bay. He knew there was plenty of fresh water falling from the sky; all he needed to do was take the bulldozer they had on hand due to nearby subway construction and push up some berms to serve as impounding dikes. It was more complicated than that, but his gentle manner and graceful hand motions reminded me of a baker explaining how he made a prize loaf by pushing it up a bit here and pulling it thus.

When he had the ponds formed, Herb Johnson worked for the remainder of his long career on embellishing the contours of his masterpiece with carefully chosen plantings. Upland birds like the bobwhite and the many varieties of warblers needed food supplies the spartina marsh would not provide. To attract them to the refuge he planted berry bushes, autumn olive, and beach plum, and on parts of the berms he sowed wheat, oats, and rye. The shorebirds would thrive on the newly protected spartina grass, which nourished an endless range of insects, crabs, and segmented worms. Within a decade, as the plantings around the refuge ponds and surrounding islands matured, the number of bird species in and around the refuge doubled. No glossy ibis, to name one magnificent example, had been observed in its gliding passage across the bay for ninety years before the refuge opened. But by the mid-sixties there were a few nesting pairs and more to follow.

Herb Johnson created an immensely successful refuge under one of the world's busiest airplane flyways. Its existence in the otherwise abused and polluted Jamaica Bay became a beacon to environmentalists everywhere, a demonstration that it was not too late to save the nation's diminishing coastal estuarine environment.

In the 1960s, in an effort to preserve major barrier islands of the East Coast from voracious real estate development and mindless urban sprawl, Congress passed legislation creating the National Seashores, a new category of national parks. These include Cape Cod, Fire Island, Assateague-Chincoteague, Cape Hatteras, Cape Kennedy, Padre Island, and others, forming a chain of extremely popular "natural area parks" along our otherwise heavily settled and commercialized coastline. In the early 1970s, at the urging of inspired urban environmentalists with political savvy (Republican mayor John Lindsay of New York, Democratic congressmen Phil Burton of San Francisco and William Fitz Ryan of New York, Marion Heiskell of the New York Parks Council, Stanley Tankel and Kim Norton of the Regional Plan Association, the biologist René Dubos, and many others), a Republican president and a Democratic Congress created yet another category of national park, the Urban National Recreation Area. The first two prototypes were Gateway in the outer harbor of New Jersey and New York, and Golden Gate in

San Francisco and surrounding bay islands. Their mission was "to preserve and protect for the enjoyment of present and future generations" the natural and historic resources within these major metropolitan regions and to "bring national parks to the people" inside the concrete cities, people who otherwise had little opportunity to visit the crown jewels of Yosemite, Glacier, Grand Canyon, and Yellowstone.

Too soon after the lobbying and organizing that created urban national recreation areas, fiscal conservatives of the Reagan era challenged the federal role in metropolitan parks. Gateway has, in consequence, never received from Washington the money needed to realize plans for its full development. But at places like Canarsie Pier and the Wildlife Refuge, the movement accomplished a great deal nonetheless. When the National Park Service began working in Jamaica Bay in 1973, outside the smaller wildlife refuge area, its crews dragged out from the marshes the hulks of over four hundred abandoned, rusted, stripped, stolen, and demoralizing automobiles. In Jamaica Bay the federal government now has jurisdiction over everything from fiddler crabs and piping plovers to food fishermen on the bridges.

I WAS AWAKENED AT daybreak by the muffled thrumming of a boat engine. Curious to see who was on the bay so early, I wormed out of the sleeping bag and stumbled on deck. About fifty yards into the liminal glimmer of morning, a bayman in a battered whaler was pulling eelpots. He had a long string of traps set along the edge of the marsh in places where the eels feed on falling debris from the marsh grasses. I remembered meeting this man many years before when he was already supplementing his seasonal construction worker's income with the work he loved most on the bay, work that allowed him to be alone in a boat. There was no substantial market for these small bay eels here in the States, except for some species used for bait. But the Japanese loved them, and exporters rushed full boxes of squirming Jamaica Bay eels by JFK air freight to Tokyo and Osaka. Human ecology is so often about the forces of desire working at a great distance. The Japanese cook who prepared a sumptuous eel dish was also warming the Irish stew on the table of a Broad Channel construction worker who would have loved to be making his entire living out on the bay.

While firing the coals on the outdoor stove, I heard another motor approaching. The wind earlier was at a steady eight knots, just sufficient to chase away the invisible but vicious marsh gnats. The air was heavy. The early sun failed to cook away the damp mist of another annoying New York day, hazy, hot, humid, with a good chance of showers. Out of the pale yellow mist came another working skiff. This one was a battered open-decked Garvey, a Paumonok classic, its outboard motor skimming it along the channel with no wake. A friendly bait digger was aboard, another young Broad Channel father on his way along the marsh to a good worming spot to spend a few hours before work digging for sand worms and blood worms. A sliced blood worm gushes deep red blood over everything. Sand worms bleed less profusely, but they have pincers that can stick a little kid, and a thousand waving scary feet. Every so often on our family outings, with all the cousins aboard, the kids caught real fish with those worms, big flounders, sometimes in a rush of bites, tangles, and scaly deck flopping, a memorable thrill well worth the trouble of cutting the bait for them.

The worm hunter waved at me and my breakfast preparations. We exchanged the look that says "This is the life." Far off on the Cross Channel Bridge, which bisects the refuge and the village of Broad Channel, I could just make out the shapes of fishermen clustered in the early morning damp, hoping to fill a pail for dinner back in the neighborhoods of central Brooklyn. A flight of ducks landed nearby, a pair of American coots from the colony that has been making the bay its permanent home. Behind the Cross Channel Bridge a silver subway train began the passage over the trestle that spans the bay behind Broad Channel.

The National Oceanographic and Atmospheric Administration's weather radio station had promised rain later in the morning. It began in earnest as I was finishing breakfast on deck. I quickly cleaned up and retreated into *Tradition*'s cabin for some further rest and reflection.

My repose was immediately disrupted by the steady drip of rain seeping through *Tradition*'s hatch carlings. These are the beams that run perpendicular to the cabin's deck beams and form the hatch opening. They were old and punky, in need of full replacement. For years I had been stuffing them with miracle goops that could never fully staunch the flow. Fortunately the rain water fell into the bilge and left the main bunk wide, warm, and cozy. Drowsy despite all the breakfast coffee, I fought sleep with little resolve. This was indeed the life, a nap after breakfast on a gently rocking bunk. But the cry of gulls circling the bay mingled with the more distant shriek of the subway and reminded me of human screams from a violent shore. I shuddered and drew the sleeping bag around my shoulders.

FINGERS OF JAMAICA BAY extend far under and beyond the concrete and steel surfaces of the Belt Parkway. They flow around the fuel tank farms of JFK International and into the Five Towns of Nassau County. The bay channels drain Marine Park, where baseball rules and Joe Torre is king; they crenellate the Rockaways with small creeks and swampy rivulets. Almost everywhere these urban bay channels are massively tamed with expensive seawalls, stone rip raps, and high earth berms where tall reed grasses (Phragmytes) flourish in place of the rich spartina of the original bay habitats. But the channels flow nonetheless, into scores of communities that border the bay.

Up in the filled wetlands well above the Belt, almost directly to the north from where *Tradition* was anchored, fingers of the bay push into East New York below Ocean Hill and Brownsville. For most of the seventies and eighties, after the rapid flight of factories and the torching of unprofitable residential properties, this area of south-central Brooklyn was one of those infamous urban war zones like the South Bronx. After years of neighborhood reconstruction, East New York was on the rebound, but there was still no lack of poverty or racial segregation in its densely populated African-American, Hispanic, and West Indian neighborhoods. Razor-wire fences and concrete-block housing projects were some of the most ubiquitous features of the landscape. My brother Pete was a veteran teacher at Transit Technology High School, which sits on the filled and graded former wetlands of East New York. For decades the school was known as East New York Vocational and was considered a failing ghetto school. Even after successful efforts to improve its performance, far too many of its students were alienated and angry. As a daily fare my brother sweated over the basics of English grammar and composition, and fought to keep order in his classes. For reward he had the talented student who wrote a prizewinning poem in the city competition and the satisfaction of knowing that many of his students each year are continuing their educations in the city's public university. I loved most his stories about coaching the annual Transit Tech entries in the Brooklyn high schools' Shakespeare festival.

As I relaxed in *Tradition*'s cabin, listening to the rain tapping on the deck above my head, I imagined Pete listening to a thin, intense teenage Othello and a glistening Desdemona with an elaborate African hairdo: *"Put out the light, and then put out the light. If I quench thee, thou flaming minister. . . ."*

When the bays of the lower harbor were a land of Dutch farms, the vast spartina wetlands were dotted with tiny settlements. Among them were Weeksville above the Jamaica Bay grasslands, Prince's Bay on Staten Island, and Communipaw on the Jersey side of the Hudson. These villages and the farms around them were populated by the Dutch, their slaves and former slaves, and probably by some Canarsie Indian stragglers who had intermingled with the Africans. In his semi-serious history of colonial New York, Washington Irving wrote that in Old New Amsterdam

> on a clear still summer evening, you may hear, from the Battery of New York, the obstreperous peals of broad-mouthed laughter of the Dutch negroes at Communipaw, who, like most other negroes, are famous for their risible powers. . . . These negroes, in fact, like the monks of the dark ages, engross all the knowledge of the place, and being infinitely more adventurous and more knowing than their masters, carry on all the foreign trade; making frequent voyages to town in canoes loaded with oysters, buttermilk, and cabbages. They are great astrologers, predicting the different changes of weather almost as accurately as an almanac; they are moreover exquisite performers on three-stringed fiddles; in whistling they almost boast of the far-famed powers of Orpheus' lyre.

Irving also recounted that the Africans and their progeny were unsurpassed at mental arithmetic, "at casting up accounts upon their fingers," and were regarded "with as much veneration as were the disciples of Pythagoras of yore." Nor is Irving fanciful in his description of the African-American presence on the waterways. From *Black Jacks,* a brilliant history by W. Jeffrey Bolster, we learn that thousands of African-American seamen, many with sea backgrounds gained on estuaries like Jamaica Bay and Raritan Bay, or in the whaling industry, were impressed during the War of 1812 into the British navy to fight against the upstart Americans. Thousands of white and African-American sailors refused to serve, the latter mainly due to fear of losing their tenuous claims to citizenship in the new democracy. The African-American rebels were imprisoned with white American sailors in England's Dartmoor prison. They were packed in segregated barracks, but there was a great deal of interaction among the prisoners. Led by heroic boxing champion "King" Richard Crafus, the boxing, dancing, fencing, writing, and reading schools of the African-American prisoners were considered the best and most enjoyable ways to pass prison time. "In No 4 the Black's Prison," a white sailor wrote, "I have spent considerable of my time, for . . . they have reading writing, Fencing, Boxing Dancing & many other schools which is very diverting to a young Person, indeed their is more amusement in this Prison than in all the rest of them." One of the chief amusements was theater, including many Shakespearean productions.

How did it happen that by Pete's childhood and mine there were relatively few African-Americans working at the better sea trades and in the more skilled and lucrative construction trades of New York and in so many other eastern ports? How were their original connections to the sea and the harbor and to good jobs in the construction trades lost or severely constricted for so long? New School professor Terry Williams, who has thoroughly researched this question, writes that in New York a part of the answer has to do with pollution of the lower bays. By mid-century the rich but polluted shellfish beds were all closed. The African-American captains and crews who manned the graceful oyster sailing sloops and who spoke to Joseph Mitchell about life in the heyday of the fishery were forgotten, ancient history.

When Pete and I were growing up, our dinner table was a running seminar on these ideas, with a special emphasis on New York City cultures and politics with all its deadly moments and low comedy. Our father for many years wrote what he called "daily doggerel," in which he satirized the endless competition, negotiation, self-promotion, and group loyalties. The building trades were dominated by "father-and-son unions," he would explain. The jobs on the tugs were passed along in tight family patterns—the precious seamen's cards were distributed among close kin. A man wanted to pass his occupation on to his sons if they chose to follow him in a trade. He fought collectively not only to raise the pay and status of the work, but to control who gets into it in the first place. To flourish or even to exist in the city, we learned, groups fought to command the economic and political niches where jobs and respect could be counted on at least to some degree. African-American migrants during the great war mobilizations won tenuous niches in transportation on the railroads, as porters at the airports, as longshoremen on some docks, and as tunnel miners (sandhogs), but their entry into most of the maritime trades and occupations was barred, just as their choice of where they might settle and live was shaped by local histories of violent racism, a history that is living. Racism explains much about how things are around Jamaica Bay, East New York, Brownsville, and many other parts of the city.

From its origin in the Bronx, the A train clatters through Harlem and midtown Manhattan over the Williamsburg Bridge and down through Brooklyn until it reaches Jamaica Bay at Howard Beach and then Broad Channel Island, before arriving along the Far Rockaways on the Atlantic beaches. While I worked on the Gateway plan, acts of racism were a feature of the daily life in the communities around Jamaica Bay. Some remain etched painfully in my memory. In 1979, for example, three white Broad Channel teenagers who were angry about having been caught earlier in jumping the turnstile at the A train stop, poured gasoline into the subway token booth on the island and immolated two token collectors, one an African-American. Then in 1986 came what then Mayor Koch called "the most horrendous incident of violence in the nine years I have been mayor." Shouting "Nigger, you don't belong here," a band of about twelve white teenagers from Howard Beach attacked and savagely beat three black men who were having a pizza on Cross Bay Boulevard. One man, Michael Griffith, was severely injured and then chased into incoming traffic on the Belt Parkway, where he was struck and killed by a car. This Howard Beach lynching was actually the second such incident that evening.

Earlier a band of Howard Beach hoodlums had beaten two Latino men, who escaped with serious but nonfatal injuries.

Those acts of violence were only the most sensational among hundreds of incidents. The racial and territorial sentiments of white communities along the bay shores made it extremely difficult to bring national parks to the people of central Brooklyn, who needed to pass through hostile white neighborhoods in order to get to places like Floyd Bennett Field and the Jamaica Bay Wildlife Refuge. Over time, though, Gateway and its neighbors have worked at resolving conflicts in the interest of the bay and its uses.

One day while we were struggling to apply the complex federal environmental planning process to urban Gateway, I went with Herb Cables, soon to become Gateway superintendent, to an informal meeting with some Broad Channel men. They wanted to discuss Gateway and Jamaica Bay and invited us to what was then the unofficial city hall of Broad Channel village, the Grassy Point Lounge on Cross Bay Boulevard. As leader of the planning team's community relations work, Cables was also our chief "flak catcher." A strikingly handsome and athletic African-American man, Herb radiated self-assurance and the desire to listen and cooperate. Our host in the tavern that day was Dan Munday, an articulate firefighter, a home and dock owner, a Broad Channel patriarch. The meeting was his idea. Its purpose was to introduce us to the thoughts and feelings of Broad Channel's baymen. He hoped that by inviting us into the informally "white only" bar we could begin to break down barriers to a relationship that could benefit both sides. The Broad Channel residents owned their bay houses and docks but had no official titles to the marshy land on which they stood. For decades they had been paying ground rent and they hoped creation of the National Recreation Area would lead the city to grant them property titles. The park planners knew that Gateway would bring a new level of law enforcement and environmental control to life on the bay and needed the cooperation of the Broad Channel residents, especially the baymen.

In the smoky blue air of the bar, with country-and-western music on the jukebox, we listened to the Broad Channel men describe their resentment of outsiders who thought they knew what was best for Jamaica Bay. They told stories about growing up in the marshes, about learning all the best fishing spots, and about picnicking with their families in secret places on the shores of the hummocks. We tried to assure them that our plans for the park would respect their superior knowledge of the bay and their concern for its preservation.

A few weeks after that meeting we circulated a draft plan. A key map showed a zoning plan for all the park's lands and waters. The islands and hummocks of Jamaica Bay were all classified as environmentally sensitive and zoned for the most stringent wilderness protection. We held public meetings about the plan all over the city, but the most surprising one occurred in Jamaica Bay itself, at a large meeting room on Floyd Bennett Field. About two hundred irate fishermen, mostly Broad Channel residents, showed up to tell us what idiots we were and to boo us off the platform. They threatened riot and mayhem, and the air in the packed meeting room smelled of alcohol. Our stupidity had been immediately visible to them. The zoning map seemed to bar them from their beloved picnicking spots and the shorelines where they dug bait and set eelpots. As Cables tried to settle the crowd and explain our intentions, I heard only angry shouts and some bitterly racist remarks from the crowd. Herb stood his ground. Dan Munday and a few of the men we had met at the Grassy Point Lounge huddled with him for a few minutes while a hush fell over the crowd. Cables then announced to the crowd that we would immediately redraw the Jamaica Bay zoning map to protect Canarsie Pol and other precious hummocks while ensuring their traditional uses of the shorelines in dispute. Dan Munday shook Cables' hand, and the cheering crowd began filing out of the room.

Herb Cables later became a high official in the Department of Interior and a fierce proponent in Washington of urban national parks. Dan Munday remained in Broad Channel, where he continued to explore the bay and advocate its use and restoration. Retired from the fire department, in the last few years he has called attention to a disturbing trend in the bay. The marshlands are eroding, and every year veteran baymen like Munday are seeing less and less healthy marsh grass, less habitat for migrating and resident birds. No one yet understands whether the loss of marsh is caused by local effects of global warming, or polluting runoff from surrounding streets, or overproduction of some mussel species on the marshes. Theories abound, and Jamaica

Bay's chief biologist, Dr. John Tanacredi, worries that it could take years to find appropriate corrective measures, further proof that we know far less than we think we do about resilience and stress in our estuaries.

MY SECOND MORNING ON Jamaica Bay began before sunrise, and by nine o'clock I was having a second breakfast. The wind was extremely light, less than five knots, the sky was hazy, and the sun failed to penetrate the damp air that seemed to hang in sheets over the silken water. Rowing in our municipal dawn, I met with the American oystercatcher, which I always identified as Susan's bird from our home marshes around Sea Dog Creek near Point Lookout. In one of Susan's poems the oystercatcher's beak is a "shard of fiery sunrise," its "throaty gurgle laps the shore, whispers through the reeds and wakes the grass."

From her perch on *Tradition*'s cabin house, Susan loved to spot this shorebird's squat body, its strong legs and dark back. My oystercatcher that morning darted along the green fringe of the wetlands and dipped a flashing beak in the sand to snag an oyster. Only recently, the *Science Times* carried an article revealing that the oystercatcher may also be a polygamous or polyandrous bird. At least his Dutch cousins are, and now ornithologists are looking into the sexual mores of our own American oystercatcher. For me, in my ancient monogamy, the oystercatcher was a reminder of Susan, and I missed her deep laughter.

Then a curtain of fire dropped on me in the form of nearly

invisible biting gnats. At intervals ravenous green horseflies dove with ferocious speed to bite an ankle. The wind was almost still, only now and then gathering into a humid puff. This gave the gnats time to assemble in clouds for a mass attack. My situation was hopeless. I was breathing gnats and fanning them from my ears.

I hurried from Pumpkin Patch Marsh with my skin on fire and motor-sailed through the channels, defeated. Here and there on the marshy edge of a hummock grocery bags fluttered like plastic foliage, a beer can glinted silver in the sand at water's edge. Lacking Dan Munday's long-term perspective, I could not see marsh erosion, and there were birds galore, the hordes of fierce flying insects their sustenance. The hummocks and islands are an avian nesting paradise. Later in the season mosquito clouds rise over the marshes and the cry goes up from backyards in Neponsit and Belle Harbor and Bergen Basin and Howard Beach and Woodmere and Hammels, and from all the Rock-aways and Canarsie, to spray the buggers and carve long drain-age ditches into the marshes. There are tense meetings among the officials about health and pesticides.

By five o'clock, after I had explored a few other bay channels, *Tradition*'s red sail was neatly furled. There was no activity on her broad decks. Docked tidily at Frank Abbracciamento's Restaurant on Canarsie Pier, she was secured again to that lovely wooden dock. It was one of those hazy, hot and humid af-ternoons of a too-suddenly warm late spring, but we were well out of the smog and humidity. Susan came by taxi from Dead

Horse Bay, where she had parked the car. We planned to wait for another hour or so in the hope that the heat would be broken by an evening breeze. Then we'd take off in the boat, after some seafood pasta at Frank's, for a sunset sail around Floyd Bennett Field to Dead Horse Bay before going home. Meanwhile we were inside the restaurant, enjoying the air-conditioning, having a cool drink, looking out over the steamy expanse of Jamaica Bay through the restaurant's wide and tinted windows.

4 / *Into the Narrows*

Probably the largest mammal definitely recorded within
the city limits in the past century was a young Sperm
Whale (Physeter catodon) that apparently had lost its
mother, followed a steamer into New York Harbor, and
suffered an untimely death when it became stranded in
Brooklyn's famous Gowanus Canal.

—John Kieran, *The Natural History of New York City*

*E*ntering the New York harbor from Jamaica Bay is not the most spectacular Atlantic Ocean approach to the city. It lacks the drama of rounding Sandy Hook (the finger of sand New Jersey gives to the harbor) from the south and seeing Manhattan suddenly appear as distant Oz, miles away but suspended over an undulating prairie of waves. On the approach into Lower New York Bay from Jamaica Bay, rounding Norton's Point and Brooklyn's Gravesend Bay, low hills at the Narrows block a clear view of the upper harbor. But even though Manhattan is hidden from view, the towers and suspended arch of the Verrazano-Narrows Bridge and the rolling hills of Staten Island and Brooklyn's Fort Hamilton offer a green and graceful welcome from the open seas.

Some weeks had passed since my cruise into the interior of Jamaica Bay, but I had managed to steal an afternoon here and there for some fussing about on *Tradition*. I had charged her batteries, secured her mast wedges, and fretted over her carburetor and its chronic colic without great success. Her tanks and coolers were full, and there was plenty of food and drink in her lockers. We were as ready as we could be for an invasion of Manhattan's concrete shores.

On this voyage into the Narrows, Susan and I were accompanied by shipmates Phil and Jules, our friends from earliest college days. Both are tolerant of *Tradition*'s quirks and of my foibles as captain, and they are rather easily distracted by a good joke or a nap.

Morning brought us perfect weather, a moderate breeze from the southwest and friendly seas. Off Norton's Point after passing Coney Island, the cry of gulls and the gongs of channel markers urged us on. But the array of markers indicating all the different channels of the lower bay was somewhat confusing, even after making the passage many times before, so we had the harbor charts open on deck ready for easy consultation. A rusted and lonely freighter flying a Liberian flag was anchored at the entrance to Gravesend Bay, which we would pass once the tide became favorable.

Jules and I agreed that the water that day was much clearer than it was in our Brooklyn and Queens childhoods, free of floating tar and feces balls, there were only drowning plastic bags and floating bits of Styrofoam. Working birds, primarily gulls and diving terns, surrounded us on every quarter. In the distance, looking southwest toward the Jersey Highlands, party fishing boats headed out of Sheepshead Bay to join others from the numerous Jersey ports in search of bluefish and flounder. Towering red nuns and green can buoys marked this world-class entrance into the New York harbor, while other buoys bore off toward the Raritan or to the smaller channels leading along the Rockaways or into Sheepshead and Jamaica Bays.

We kept *Tradition* on a southwest course, taking long tacks across a breeze blowing over the Atlantic Highlands and Sandy Hook. This was the inner part of the New York Bight. We crossed the southern edges of treacherous Romer Shoal, heading for the Sandy Hook Channel after crossing the deep Ambrose Channel at the green can buoy #3, which we spotted in the bright sun with no trouble. Romer Shoal, sometimes called "the Lump," is famous among harbor people as a spot where at low tide the water can be as shallow as four feet. These shoals are reminders of how important the massive dredging operations have been to the existence of the commercial port.

The New York and New Jersey harbor complex now ranks fourth in ocean vessels arriving in U.S. ports, behind Houston, New Orleans and Los Angeles/Long Beach. Still, with close to five thousand ships entering the Narrows each year, to say nothing of the many ferries, tugs with tows, large government ships, and work vessels, the Narrows can be as busy a shipping lane as one would ever wish to sail through. It is routine to see a line of tankers extending out to the horizon and steaming toward the Ambrose Channel, or to encounter two or three anchored at the mouth of Gravesend Bay, awaiting a favorable tide or open berth.

Nowadays most ships are maneuverable enough to come up into the lower bay and through the Narrows under their own steam. For most of its history, however, the lower bay was the realm of the "hookers." In 1938, a year before I was born, a veteran tug captain described for A.J. Libeling what port traffic was like during his youth on the hooker tug *Leonard Richards* at the end of the age of sail:

What was a Hooker? Why a tug that cruised off Sandy Hook for schooners, of course. Just the same as a Gater was a tug that hanged off Hell Gate, and a Lugger was a tug that lugged ships to their births after the Hookers and the Gaters brought them in, whether the ships was pine wooders from the South or brickers, or whatever they might be.

Them days there was more ships than now, and plenty of sail. The most part of them had no regular agents ashore to hire tugs, and there was no radio, anyway, so the agents wouldn't a'knowed when they was coming in. The first tug that seed a ship he made up to her and the two captains paced their deck awhile and called each other this and that and at last they struck a bargain, or they didn't, and you sheered off and he run up the American flag for another tug.

Captain Joe was describing the port when West and South Streets in lower Manhattan's financial district were booming dock areas with ships and boats of every description, motor and sail. The hooker tugs worked the outer harbor and near ocean reaches, a section of the New York Bight I think of now as the Gateway Triangle. There are three wonderful recreational sailing ports there, each forming the apex of an almost equilateral triangle: Dead Horse Bay at the entrance to Jamaica Bay; Sandy Hook, about nine sailing miles to the southwest; and Great Kills Harbor on Staten Island, nearer to the Narrows and the Verrazano Bridge. All three of these ports are easily accessible from the ocean or from the upper bay and the East River or the Hudson. Each offers excellent free anchorages or ample dockage with easy access to nearby services, restaurants, and mass transit; in other words, the works for the metropolitan cruiser. All three are within Gateway National Recreation Area. From any of these ports it isn't a long sail into the upper bay, or into Raritan Bay and from there up the Kills behind Staten Island into the busy commercial ports of New Jersey.

My original plan was to sail across the mouth of the lower bay to Spermaceti Cove on Sandy Hook for some first-class nature watching and lunch. We'd catch the beginning of a flood tide in the early afternoon and head up into the Narrows and the city, where we would try to put in at Battery Park City in lower Manhattan to let off Phil and Jules. Then we'd anchor for the night in the flats by the Statue of Liberty and Ellis Island, and the next day Susan and I would continue up the East River on the flood tide. We had started off later than I had hoped, however, so I decided against trying for Sandy Hook. Instead we made long tacks in the lower bay while we waited for the tide at the Narrows to turn in our favor.

In my personal geography, this was the grandest region of our home waters. *Tradition,* and the people sprawled in her cockpit, were a tiny blip in the ocean on the edge of America. Depending on the tides, the Atlantic either surges up the Hudson or pulls away the fluids and silt of the interior. We made little headway against an ebb tide rushing the waters of the Hudson and all the surrounding bays out through the Narrows. The breeze moderated to a vesper and failed to stir more than a trickle of sea over the rudder. We were lulled into a torpid silliness by the undulations of wave and the sun's warmth. In two hours or so we knew that the flood tide would help push us through the Narrows under the bridge, but at that moment Manhattan was still a faraway island. In the near distance, below the bridge, Forts Hamilton and Wadsworth pretended to guard the Narrows against intruders; they've never fired a shot in anger, although during the world wars a submarine net was slung between them to protect the upper bay from German U-boats.

We were sailing along the course to Golden America traced by waves of sea-weary immigrants and wide-eyed explorers before them. Jules remarked that we were sailing into the harbor on a "ya-chet," a puny one filled with the children and grandchildren of immigrants. My grandparents, Susan's grandparents,

Jules' parents, and Phil himself with his mother and brothers came into this same harbor as immigrant greenhorns on crowded steamers. The sight of their children and grandchildren sailing in small boats out in the ocean, like Commodore Vanderbilt in his fancy yachts, could have been only a dream. But with the exception of Phil, the actual immigrant, we know almost nothing of our Middle European roots, obliterated by holocaust. Our ancestors were wave-tossed on these shores. Our inheritance is the city and the port.

A whitecap broke with a swoosh against *Tradition*'s bow. A glint of sunlight struck something in the water: a bluefish slapping through a translucent wave. To the southwest, above the Jersey Highlands, an alarming thunderhead soared above a darkening sky. Slants of sun played over the rising seas and gusts of renewed wind delivered the steady chatter of terns, then the deep mourn of a ship's signal horn. The breeze from the southwest had freshened, and now it blew almost directly from our original Sandy Hook destination. This is the beauty of the Gateway ports in the lower bay: there is one for almost any weather condition. An excellent point of sail would take us out of the ship channels onto the shallower water toward Great Kills on the nearer shores of Staten Island, and we headed *Tradition* that way. Her Dutch red sail billowed out on a powerful broad reach and she plowed over the whitecaps, her spars arched against the wind gusts, her snugly cleated mainsheet almost humming with the strain. The boat was singing and we were singing: "A Capital ship for an ocean trip, was a walloping window blind, no wind that blew dismayed her crew or troubled the captain's mind . . . (HA)."

As soon as we were caught up in the delight of outrunning the whitecaps off our stern quarter, I heard a warning from the bilge. The slosh of water told me the bilge pump was clogged — not dangerous, just an annoying demand for attention. Susan was dozing in the sun, so Jules relieved me at the helm.

The bilge, the lowest place on the boat, was down below under the box step leading into the cabin. Small bits of rotted wood, pieces of *Tradition,* were clogging the intake and swirling around in the bilge. As the boat heeled with the wind, even at the conservative fifteen or so degrees that a catboat heels, the water drained from the low places into the bilge in a swirl of fouled sea and rain water. I easily unclogged the intake hose but had to sit for a while with the pump to make sure that more pieces did not reclog the system, that we weren't "pumping the boat out" with the bilge water. The fundamental flaw of a restoration job in which fiberglass has merely been layed over the hull of an old wooden vessel, however well and thick, is that over time the boat rots from the inside under the plastic. I was pumping the old boat out, piece by piece, in the semidarkness of the low-pitched cabin while my friends tended to the sailing.

Then I felt an altering of our course. *Tradition* had turned somewhat downwind and we were running along the waves, off course. I poked my head up to see that Jules had become distracted by some deep thought or problem. An engineer, computer scientist, and financial wizard, and a practical man at most times, Jules is given to pondering the intangibles of life or the physical universe at odd moments, of which this was one; we were well off course. Phil had followed Susan's lead and was napping. Just as I was about to warn Jules to bring the boat further into the wind, an errant gust caught the leeward edge of the sail. I shouted a warning. Too late. A massive jibe threw the boom across the boat. Twenty-six feet of wooden spar and yards of heavy sail swept across the deck and snapped against the sheet, all the way over on the opposite tack. The force of the swinging boom tore the sheet block off its fitting on the boom. Phil and Jules were lost in a spaghetti tangle of limp rope and blocks. The boom was suspended aloft by the topping lift, unable to actually harm anyone on deck unless they happen to be standing up, but we no longer had control of the boom and sail, which were flying and flapping far beyond the port side of the boat. Waves caught us almost broadside and rolled everyone around a good deal.

Before I could reach the wheel, a startled Susan had taken over with a few salty expletives. She used *Tradition*'s remaining forward motion to point her into the wind while she started the engine. With the boat headed upwind, she brought the sail back over the deck where we could immediately secure the boom and sail with a spare line. Jules and Phil gathered the sheet and blocks to begin untangling the difficulty. The fitting at the boom was snapped clean and not repairable. Since repairs would take some time and preferably some calm, we made for the entrance to Great Kills Harbor. Susan stayed at the helm while we downed the sail, made it fast to the boom with a few sail stops, and secured the boom in its crutch. We were about twenty minutes from the harbor entrance. The motor moved *Tradition* smartly onward, but under its rhythmic throbbing I heard the occasional hiccup of the fouled carburetor, a reminder of the need for more extensive repairs later.

We threaded our way past a small flotilla of flounder fishermen drifting outside the mouth of Great Kills Harbor and anchored just inside Crookes Point, a former island now connected to the mainland by dredging spoil, a wetland promontory with low-lying vegetation, a place popular with solitary fishermen and serious birders. Great Kills is a secluded harbor, one of the better kept secrets of the New York Bight, with an anchorage like a large pond surrounded by wetlands protected by the Park Service. Close by stands a quiet Staten Island village neighborhood with modest private homes like my native Flushing and other New York City villages from earlier in the century. Great Kills is perfectly located: birds galore, services at dockside in the adjacent neighborhood, bus service along Hylan Boulevard to all points, and a wide beach for sunning, swimming, cookouts, and walks along the beach with views of the Narrows or the wide ocean. In this new calm, Susan gently teased Jules about the disjuncture between his immense mathematical and theoretical abilities and his span of attention. We banished Phil to the galley, where he could turn his years of professional hash-slinging to good use. Hunched over the galley's two-burner alcohol stove, he put the galley into cramped but serviceable shape. Soon we could smell a pot of chicken soup bubbling on the fire, and Phil started handing up sandwiches from below.

After lunch the crew lazed on deck while I finished the necessary rigging repairs. One of the joys of maintaining a decrepit workboat is scavenging through old hardware in one of the disappearing nautical junk stores along the shore, looking for fittings that may come in handy at moments like these. Yachty turnbuckles, which cost seventy-five dollars or more in bronze or stainless steel, can be found in galvanized steel for ten dollars, or perhaps three dollars in decent used condition. The same goes for shackles, lag bolts, screw eyes, nuts, and washers. The bottom of my toolbox was a tangled nest of these fittings. I quickly made the necessary repairs to *Tradition*'s boom and sheet block, and we were again ready to up anchor. But then the thunderstorm approached.

The time between distant thunder and lightning strokes warned us the storm was about half an hour away. We could see the looming gray clouds as they came over the hills of Staten Island, but they had lost some of their earlier menace and promised no more than an early summer afternoon squall and shower. Sunlit margins of sky limited the storm on either side of the dark clouds, so I recommended that we resume our cruise into Upper New York bay. The flood tide had begun almost an hour earlier and would push us easily through the Narrows and under the bridge. We would have plenty of time on a favorable tide if we merely wanted to reach the Battery or thereabouts. If we decided to move farther up the river we would need a longer time on the fair tide. These were my arguments in favor of making way despite the gathering storm. Led by Susan, the opposition raised fears of lightning, the possibilities of squall conditions, danger of the unknown, fear of acting imprudently, reminders of the lesson of the luckless *Castel Del Rey,* questions about the captain's judgment, and so on. The local weather radio report noted the storm's position in the lower bay over the Jersey Shore but played down its significance. This information strengthened my authority as captain. Against Susan's persistent warnings, we upped anchor and quit the snug security of Great Kills for the more open seas and swifter currents of the lower bay.

As soon as we cleared the last of the buoys marking the narrow channel into Great Kills Harbor, *Tradition* plowed into a steep chop. For the first time all day we took some spray over the bow, and it was time to break out the slickers. We were terribly spoiled on our beamy vessel, which despite her low freeboard and consequent proximity to the choppy surface parted the waters evenly.

Over Staten Island's South Beach and the lovely green hills above it loomed a narrow wall of purple clouds. White gulls and gray-silver terns veered in the updraft like feathered particles in a vast bubble chamber. Wind gusts from the west-southwest billowed *Tradition's* double-reefed sail. Water boiled along her stern, and we again felt the lifting power of her sail and curving spars. The boat made close to her hull speed, almost six knots, two more knots contributed by the flood tide. Sped along with this wind and fair tide, we would reach the Verrazano-Narrows Bridge well within an hour. A single lightning bolt fractured the purple cloud bank, its thunder muffled in the whistling breeze. *Tradition* sped along on an exhilarating reach for about twenty minutes, passing over Old Orchard Shoals parallel to Staten Island's New Dorp and South Beaches.

Off the shore, well before the bridge, Swinburne and Hoffman Islands appeared before us as two green and desolate lumps. Those islands, neither more than about five acres in area, were built largely from construction landfill and were among the port's early centers for disease control. Always sensitive to the temptation of other New Yorkers to treat their fair shores as dumping grounds for the larger city's sanitation and health problems, Staten Islanders protested against the expansion of infectious disease quarantine centers on their island, so in 1872 the authorities relented and built up two small islands off South Beach, islets of landfill for gloomy isolation hospitals. During the heyday of immigration early in the twentieth century, these were major hospitals where many hopeless immigrant children and adults died of TB, typhus, and yellow fever. Hoffman and Swinburne are just two of the many islands in the urban archipelago that were once used to store the cast-off, diseased, and dying of the tenement quarters. At one time almost all the smaller islands in New York Bay or on the rivers have seen their loneliness used to the advantage of public hygiene and exile.

Against the gray skies of the coming squall, Hoffman and Swinburne were conversation killers, their shallow ruins thick with scraggly sumac trees and poison ivy. As part of Gateway National Recreation Area, the federal rangers defend their solitude and exclusive use by nonhuman species. Nesting double-crested cormorants are now among the islands' most notable tenants. On my first visit to the islands in the early 1970s, it was astounding to see their rocky shores littered with piles of bleached chicken bones and dry bone shards of devoured pork chops. At that time the city was still moving garbage barges around the harbor to active landfills on Staten Island and elsewhere. Above every departing tug with its sad tow of messy barges there circled a riot of gulls in a diving frenzy. The islands were a convenient picnic ground for their quarrelsome gull feasts, and so, with some exaggeration, I think of Hoffman and Swinburne as the chicken bone reefs.

We were sailing close to them, on the shoal side of the Hudson's mouth and at the edge of the commercial ship channel, which at that moment was free of ocean traffic. The small-craft captain, whether under sail or power, is obliged by the strict rules of marine navigation to yield the right-of-way to large vessels that cannot maneuver outside the shipping channels. Earlier in the port's history, in the time of the luckless *Castel Del Rey*, these shoals were dangerous and dreaded. But to the small-craft sailor they are most welcome; at night, or in fog or storms, they provide some assurance (once you're sailing over them) that some great freighter, cruise ship, or tug heavily burdened with a string of barges, isn't likely to run up from behind and splinter your boat into driftwood. This particular fear is hardly irrational. Most of the standard cruising guides describe these waters as an exciting, majestic, but worrisome world port plagued by tankers and commercial shipping hazards that have to be endured on the way to or from the peaceful cruising ports of Long Island Sound. But as long as you're sure that you are out of harm's way, the sights of the commercial shipping and the memories they evoke are one of the pleasures of passage through the Narrows and, for that matter, through the entire harbor area.

I once asked Captain Hubert S. Prime, a friend of mine and a former New York harbor pilot and tug captain, what the seamen on the big commercial ships and tugs think about us recreational boaters. Captain Prime was a lover of catboats and appreciated what it meant to sail an ample but rather slow and quirky scow through the Narrows and into the upper bay. His advice to me and others was, "Do it, be careful, observe the rules, stay on the edges of the channels where possible," but by all means take advantage of the sights of the harbor and the gift of being on the waters in what he termed a "fine and well-adapted little boat."

Captain Prime and the other professional skippers encounter recreational boaters and fishermen every working day in the warm months, often in some of the tightest, most awkward spots in the harbors. I agree with Edward Hoagland that tug captains "have a special knowledge of tragedy and peril." Captain Prime often preferred to tell specific stories in response to vague questions like mine, and his favorite tale was ironic and cautionary:

I'm coming down from Newark Bay and there's this little twenty six footer. There's a bridge there at Bergen Point and this guy, instead of coming on through a span on either side of the draw, or outside in the shallow water, he headed for the main span which I was heading for. I was piloting a three hundred foot ship, a Danish ship, and here's this guy headed right for us. The capt says, "Should I blow the alarm?".

"I said to him, well, you can blow the alarm to cover the law, but he won't know what you're blowing for. These people are out of this world."

The capt blew the alarm and this guy, just at the end of the draw, his boat stalled. By this time, of course we were almost up to the draw. His boat turned sideways, and the guy he was waving like we could do something about it, come right over maybe and help him out. He had four people on the boat and they all ran up to the bow. By this time I had stopped the engines, of course, and told the Captain, Full Astern. I don't know if it was smart or not because you don't know what the ship is going to do. It could turn sideways in the draw. But we did it and later the Captain told me he had put in an Emergency Full Astern. So the four people ran up to the bow of their

little boat, and they jumped off, none wearing life preservers.

When they jumped off they gave their boat a little push.
They went down one side of the ship and their boat went
down the other. Of course as soon as they were in the water we gave the order to stop the engines. One of those
guys went down the length of the ship pushing himself
away from the side the whole way. I called the tug that
was following and I said get ready to pick some people up
because there are four in the water. I notified the Coast
Guard and also told my tug crew to get ready to take the
people back to the Moran yard and to have an ambulance
ready.

When they got back to the yard they were ok and refused any medical care. The Coast Guard got there and
there was a small work boat working near the bridge that
went and picked up the little boat. Later the Coast Guard
took them back to pick up their boat. I think that after all
it was the captain and I who were the most upset, we just
didn't know what was going to happen.

Despite his bizarre brushes with recreational boaters, Captain
Prime believed that more then ever the harbor was a wonderful
place to explore in a small boat, especially if the explorer used
some basic common sense and observed the rules of the road.

With these warnings, assurances, and cautionary tales much
on my mind, we headed quickly for the arching span of the

Verrazano-Narrows Bridge: vertical clearance 229 feet at center, no problem for *Tradition* with her 26-foot mast.

The War of 1812 fortifications on the shore of Fort Wadsworth on the Staten Island side of the bridge came into full view, and with the river channel free of shipping we slipped across to the Brooklyn shore on a starboard tack toward Fort Hamilton. We traversed the Narrows while slanting under the bridge, feeling dwarfed and humbled by its arching mass. All this traversing took us about twenty minutes, and ten that we sailed easily on a port tack along the rolling hills and generous esplanade of the Brooklyn shore. Joggers nodded in passing, and children waved excitedly. Then the darkened sky opened up with a perfectly gentle Hudson Valley thundershower. We laughed at the rain spotting our glasses. Amid the gusts of wind and rather soft thunderclaps, the lightning passed far from our vulnerable spars, and soon slants of sunlight again played everywhere on the water.

As we rounded Brooklyn at Sunset Park beyond Bay Ridge, we caught our first complete sight of the upper bay featuring Miss Liberty, Ellis Island, the Gowanus and Red Hook, the Jersey flats below the gleaming new waterfront of Jersey City, Governors Island, and then, finally, our first view of that cosmic ship berthed in the river: Manhattan, towering above the Battery and dividing the Hudson.

On our way toward Manhattan we listened to Louis Armstrong playing and singing "La Vie en Rose" and "Dream a Little Dream." *Tradition* may have been on her last legs, but she had a first-class sound system. Avoiding each other's eyes, the four of us looked silently out on our magical city encircled by water.

The idea of a sail around the statue and Ellis Island on this fair and enchafed flood (as W.H. Auden called it) was tempting, but I had a less picturesque and immediately meaningful destination: a detour into the Gowanus Canal for documentary purposes. Afterward we would skirt the waterfront edge of old Red Hook and sail along the old industrial Brooklyn shore, where we'd let the last hour or so of the flood tide carry us up the East River to the Brooklyn Bridge.

A late afternoon breeze after the gentle squall filled *Tradition*'s sail nicely. The lift of the sail and the strong current beneath her pushed the boat steadily up the Bay Ridge Channel toward the Erie Basin and the Gowanus entrance.

From out on the river, the entrance to Gowanus Canal seemed lost in a maze of waterways and looming multistoried warehouses, many belonging to the Erie Basin complex just above the canal's actual beginning. Within the cove known as Gowanus Bay, bordered by the Erie Basin, the canal itself soon narrows and disappears into the heart of old tenement neighborhoods that were undergoing rapid renewal and gentrification as the water quality in the canal improved. The city had revived a massive underwater propeller that pushed stagnant water out toward the East River and assisted the tidal action in circulating oxygenated water into the Gowanus' once fetid upper reaches.

John Waldman, an environmental scientist for the Hudson River Foundation, reports in *Heartbeats in the Muck,* his biological tour of the harbor, that in the late nineteenth and early twentieth centuries the Gowanus was the busiest commercial canal in the United States: "Much of the timber, sand, and brownstone that built modern Brooklyn passed through the Gowanus. There were foundries, slaughterhouses, cement makers, flour mills, gashouses, and other fouling enterprises along its banks." A dye works' colorful discharges inspired the nickname "Lavender Lake." It's difficult to imagine that in Brooklyn's early history there was naturally flowing water here. Local residents knew the place as Gowane's Creek, after the Canarsie Indian chief who once lived nearby. Some of the region's largest and tastiest oysters fattened in the wetlands and tributary streams of the area, but by the Civil War the creek had been ditched, its banks hardened into an industrial canal that became famous for its industrial commerce and evil stench.

By the twentieth century's end, restoration of the city's abused marine ecology was a more popular theme, and the Gowanus became a local symbol of a new urban environmental sensibility. Remnants of salt marsh appeared at the edges of abandoned bulkheads, community groups led eco-tours to marvel at nature's reclamation of the dead zone, and fisherman began working the canal's healthier outer reaches. A group of local residents formed the Gowanus Dredgers Canoe Club and began offering visitors a chance to take a paddle on the canal's quiet waters. Artists moved into old industrial lofts along the canal, harbingers of increasing property values and new investments in the surrounding neighborhoods. One of the city's most imaginative museums, the Waterfront Museum on a striking red Lehigh Valley freight barge, claimed a section of renovated pier above the canal and Erie Basin, where it commemorates the history and restoration of the port, including the Gowanus Canal, and the people who once lived here.

We tacked back and forth across the mouth of the canal in Gowanus Bay, our attention diverted by a rusted freighter, a confiscated drug ship, which leaned against a Port Authority impoundment pier, a remnant of the canal's criminal history. Al "Scarface" Capone began his career as a thug and criminal here, and in the fifties there were deadly struggles between crusading union longshoremen and Mafia thugs who bled the unions of their money and idealism. That violent history keeps resurfacing. Recently, a local fisherman, attracted to the cleaner outer reaches of the canal, hooked a suitcase from the bottom that contained not treasure but human body parts from more than one person.

We were eager to explore the canal's inner reaches, but the strong East River current kept carrying us beyond the entrance. I resolved to nose *Tradition* farther up the canal on another voyage, and we headed into Red Hook Channel on the Brooklyn side of the East River.

Across the channel, the steel-and-glass towers of lower Manhattan soared above Governors Island, but they did not beckon, at least not to me. We headed *Tradition* for Red Hook itself, on the Brooklyn side of the harbor. With a fair wind and a favorable tide, the boat sliced effortlessly through the river swells. The distant sounds of the city around us mingled with the nearer sounds of buoys and gulls, and our eyes were drawn inevitably to the coves and creeks of the decrepit Brooklyn waterfront and its evidence of new possibilities in the old neighborhoods. Cranes on high girders and the occasional barge or tug were clear evidence of work and industry on the waterfront, while the chrome and gray corporate boxes on lower Manhattan's shore spoke silently of the officebound in front of their computer screens.

For New Yorkers who have heard of it at all, the name Red Hook evokes Eva Marie Saint and Marlon Brando in *On the Waterfront* (although much of the film was shot on the Hoboken waterfront in New Jersey), the smells and sights of the decaying docklands with their deserted piers and jagged pilings, and the nostalgia of the old residents who cling to their shrinking waterfront neighborhood, bisected in classic Robert Moses style by the congested Gowanus Expressway and walled in by the Red Hook Houses. From the river, Red Hook presents its most attractive features: its waterfront and the church spires that define it as one of the original industrial villages that lined the Brooklyn-Queens shores from Bay Ridge to Flushing.

When the Italian and Irish residents of Red Hook's waterfront tenements speak of their neighborhoods, they talk of imminent death and a sense of loss, even as they cling steadfastly to their shrinking turf. "They believe," says one of my City University colleagues, sociologist Philip Kasinitz, "it is right to stay in a place where they are 'known,' even if many residents no longer know them." Their loyalties to place and to memory run deep: "I been sleeping with the Lady a long time," said one Red Hook man with a view of the Statue of Liberty from his bedroom window. Red Hook, the old-timers assert, did not just die. It was killed by larger outside forces that crushed the village. They spread blame generously, to the industries for abusing the area and closing the docks, to the Catholic archdiocese for closing the local parochial school, and so on. They blame, with special bitterness, the public-housing residents who, Kasinitz says, "despite their poverty, are seen as 'getting everything,' and the politicians who are seen as indulging them." They also view the concentration of noxious industries and waste transfer stations, which local community planning groups fought bitterly against, as evidence that the outside world continues to dump on Red Hook.

The Red Hook old-timers hardly have a monopoly on nostalgia in this harbor town. When I think of my home community of Flushing, Queens, I yearn for the magnificent cathedral alleys formed by stately elms along the avenues, before they were killed by Dutch elm disease and developers; for a time before the neighborhoods became crowded with newcomers from China, Korea, and the Indian subcontinent. But each generation fixes on scenes of its own moment on center stage, and soon the children of the newcomers will be nostalgic about the Golden

Age of hope and community in the Flushing of their youth, at the time of the millennium.

Nostalgia supports a good deal of the best in historic preservation in Brooklyn and elsewhere in the city. A yearning for the scenes of one's youth may not help to house newcomers, or stimulate new industry and arts, or address the problems of poverty and race, but in nostalgia there is often the wisdom that comes from deep attachment to the streets and physical places of a community. A classic example is from Staten Island's Mr. Hunter, who, as a young man, served as a cook for the African-American sloop captains in the oyster fishery of the lower bay. Toward the end of his life, Mr. Hunter described for Joseph Mitchell what it was like raising a family in Sandy Ground and Prince's Bay on Staten Island in the first decades of the twentieth century. He remembered that "people looked after things" then and that they were careful about their yards and their trash. They "taught their children how to conduct themselves."

And they held their heads up; they were as good as anybody, and better than some. And they got along with each other; they knew each other's peculiarities and took them into consideration. . . . Of course this was an oyster town, and there was always an element that drank and carried on and didn't have any more moderation than the cats up the alley, but the great majority were good Christians who walked in the way of the Lord and loved Him, and trusted Him, and kept His commandments.

Then, for the fishing people of Prince's Bay, "the water went bad." People began contracting typhoid fever from eating Staten Island oysters and were hustled off to ghastly isolation hospitals on the harbor's disease islands.

A few decades later, similar blows hit Red Hook's long-shoring families. The container technologies wiped out not only an economic livelihood but a way of life. There were thousands of jobs on docks and in warehouses when men were needed to move barrels, bales, cartons, and cargo of all shapes and kinds. But soon after World War II, machines moved containers directly from ships to trucks or rail cars and on to their destinations, with few men needed to "break bulk" on the piers and warehouses. The container ships also required huge cranes and cargo-moving technologies, which in turn demanded far more space than was available on the old Brooklyn waterfront. The shipping action moved to newer facilities on the Jersey side of the port. Red Hook declined quickly, its population dropping from 21,000 in the fifties to about 12,000 in the nineties. The Red Hook Houses were home to fewer longshoring families and more African-American and Latino families, without adequate work or income to make them secure or particularly welcome members of the community.

In recent years younger people have moved in, attracted by improvements in water quality, growing interest in community preservation, and the incessant search for affordable places to live and work. Among the newcomers are activists skilled at forming neighborhood organizations and building web sites, and artists and craftspeople who live and work in Red Hook or nearby communities. But positive change occurs in fits and starts. In the early nineties, a good deal of money, about $42 million, was wasted on an effort to build a modern "fishport" on the Red Hook waterfront. This gleaming new facility was supposed to replace the Fulton Fish Market in lower Manhattan and bring about seven hundred jobs into Red Hook. But too few ships and boats brought fresh fish into the harbor. More seafood was transported on ice in trucks, and the fishport —which closed six months after it opened—became another example to Red Hook's residents of bureaucratic fumbling. On a brighter note, the Port Authority's bargain sale of waterfront acreage to a local developer, Greg O'Connell, was successful. O'Connell delivered on his promise to open a half-mile of waterfront to the public. The waterfront now hosts an annual Red Hook waterfront arts festival, and his project has also attracted some small manufacturing concerns. Perhaps someday we will even see some renewed wooden boat-building activity on this stretch of the Brooklyn shore, and some places to tie up a small boat for a while.

WHILE I PONDERED THE power of community ties and nostalgia, the current carried *Tradition* well above Governors Island. We sailed farther out into the river to get a full view of the city from midstream. We were approaching the South Street Seaport on the Manhattan shore and, beyond it, the graceful Brooklyn Bridge with its spiderwork of cables, forever the first and greatest of all the East River suspension-bridge crossings. At the South Street Seaport the ships moored along the display pier were magnificently restored. From some angles the scene conveyed a living history of the waterfront, and Sloppy Louie's restaurant was still there, an authentic Fulton Fish Market institution even if the patrons these days are anything *but* sloppy. The Seaport has encouraged a revival of interest in the harbor and its life, and promotes marine restoration, harbor sailing, and much more. But to maintain its hold on prime waterfront property, it also depends on its shopping mall and food court. Keeping the shops busy demands far larger crowds than those a few old ships and a nautical museum would ever draw.

Families up on the food-court deck pointed to us out on the river and waved. We tacked back toward downtown Brooklyn, which towers above Brooklyn Heights, and continued along on the current up the East River. The sail slatted in the confusing winds and urban williwaws that suddenly blew down from the city's towers. Sometimes under power and sometimes with the help of the sail, we headed to one of my favorite spots along the river: the restored pier at Fulton Ferry Landing, the music barge, and the fancy restaurant at the foot of the Brooklyn Bridge in the center of Old Brooklyn.

This part of Brooklyn, from the bridge to the Navy Yard, figured prominently in my childhood. My maternal grandfather and uncles were ironworkers, and before World War II they worked in this part of the city on building projects. My wildly romantic Uncle Pete, the uncle closest to me and the one who introduced me to the twin addictions of sailing and seaports, worked in the Brooklyn Navy Yard as a highly skilled ship welder, before he joined the Navy Seabees in World War II. On my paternal side the men were not handy at all; my father feared using tools because he felt clumsy and incapable. But my grandfather William and his two brothers, Sam and A.J., were partners in a highly successful wholesale fruit and vegetable business in the Wallabout Market, also in this section of old Brooklyn. The market is long gone, remembered only in historic photos, and so is the Navy Yard, at least for shipbuilding and repair.

The city's planners and community leaders had struggled to adapt the riverfront for city dwellers of the global-but-sedentary information age who yearned to walk the river's edges. They succeeded with isolated stretches of the East River, especially this spot with its breathtaking views of the Brooklyn Bridge and the island across the water. Each success has stimulated new initiatives, and gradually the city's river shores have become more accessible to the public.

The old Fulton Ferry Landing was also quite near the East River shore where the British occupiers of New York, during the Revolutionary War, berthed the infamous prison ship *New Jersey*, long before construction of the Brooklyn Bridge. Writing in the early 1860s, Walt Whitman railed against the neglect of history amid the boosterism and commercial frenzy of the new democracy. He was referring specifically to American seamen and soldiers who perished in the stinking hold of the British prison ship, where thousands died tormented deaths from fever, starvation and dehydration.

> It is a profound reflection that Brooklyn, in its Wallabout region, holds the remains of this vast and silent army. . . . At that period, the spot that is now just west of the wall along Flushing Avenue was a low stretching sand hill, and it was in and adjacent to this spot that the thousands of American martyrs were mostly buried. They were dumped in loose loads every morning in pits, and the sand shoveled over them. The writer of these lines has been told by old citizens that nothing was more common in their early days than to see thereabout plenty of the skulls and other bones of these dead—and that thoughtless boys would kick them about in play. Many of the martyrs were so insecurely buried that the sand, being blown off by the wind, exposed their bleached skeletons in great numbers.

We tied *Tradition* up quite near the spot Whitman described so that we could take in the soaring view. We were between the music barge and the River Cafe on the concrete pier maintained by the Department of Parks. Lines from Whitman's "Crossing Brooklyn Ferry" are engraved in large letters on the railing that extends along the entire perimeter of the pier. Against a background of the great bridge and the Manhattan profile, people from all over the globe walk slowly along the railing to view the poetry engraved there:

Flow on, river! flow with the flood-tide, and ebb with the
ebb-tide!
Frolic on, crested and scallop-edg'd waves!
Gorgeous clouds of the sunset! drench with your splendor
me, or the men and women generations after me!
Cross from shore to shore, countless crowds of
passengers!
Stand up, tall masts of Mannahatta! stand up, beautiful
hills of Brooklyn!
Throb, baffled and curious brain! throw out questions
and answers!

After resting for a while under the bridge, we eased the boat
a few yards upriver from Fulton Ferry Landing to a small
wooden dock, where I hopped ashore at the landing owned by
the chic River Café. In contrast to the adjacent pier, which is on
steel-and-concrete pilings high above the river and has no facilities to tie up a small boat or to come ashore, the restaurant's
dock, though quite small, seemed designed for just that purpose. But since I had never seen transient boats tied up there, I
had a hunch what the answer would be. "No, I'm terribly
sorry," an elegant young hostess explained. "You can't stay at
the dock. We can't accept reservations from people on boats because we're not insured at the dock." We moved on.

At slack tide, we circled around in the suddenly still river and
admired the view of the bridge and the Manhattan shore. When
the tide was just beginning its ebb, we hitched a ride on its back

to round the Battery and made for the shore on the lower Hudson River side of Manhattan Island.

Safely past the busy ferry lanes at the tip of Manhattan, we tacked around the old Battery fire dock with its new restaurant and rode a favorable breeze on a beam reach that pushed us well against the gathering ebb tide in the Hudson. We made slow but steady progress past the Holocaust Museum and then along the concrete shores of Battery Park City, just above the historic fireboat basin and dock at the edge of Battery Park itself. Battery Park City was built, as Whitman wrote about the navy shipyards in the Wallabout, "out of old Neptune — that is, it has been filled in." We sailed parallel to the shore of Battery Park City with its ample esplanade, where Melville once described the land-tied multitudes staring out into the harbor, dreaming of voyage and adventure. Then we tacked easily into the South Cove at the southern end of the Battery Park complex. The far larger North Cove was reserved exclusively for ferries, large charter boats, and major pleasure yachts. The smaller South Cove was set up as a small-craft harbor with pilings and what seemed to be easy access to the Manhattan shore. I'd had my eye on it since it was built and hoped it would be a convenient place to tie up to discharge Phil and Jules into the city.

It was approximately six o'clock when we furled the sail, tied *Tradition* to a convenient set of pilings in the South Cove, and looked for the way up and onto shore. Three or four couples hung over the railings or meandered along the walk. Local families with children, and no doubt a smattering of domestic and international tourists, waved and smiled down at our old gaff rigger. But there was no way to get ashore. There were no steps, no dock, no ladder, no gangplank, only unbroken railing. A security guard huffed over to the edge of the cove nearest to us and waved us away with a warning that we were not permitted to stay or to discharge passengers.

Phil and Jules were up to that kind of challenge. The tide remained high enough to make it possible to reach the concrete edge of the bulkhead. After exchanging hugs and kisses, we eased the boat up to the nearest place for them to climb up and over the fence. In full view of the sputtering security guard and the curious onlookers, they easily scaled the bulkhead and the railing above it. Phil, in typical fashion, opened a large tear in the seat of a worn but much-loved pair of my pants, which he had borrowed from me just that morning.

Susan and I chose not to torment the frustrated security guard at Battery Park City, where "insurance problems" and now, sadly, the fear of terrorism explain why the South Cove is not an actual boating facility. We sailed with the ebbing tide across the Hudson to the shallow flats that surround the Statue of Liberty and Ellis Island, a good spot to anchor for the night in full view of the entire port, out of the heavily trafficked deep waters. Under the protective arm of nearby Miss Liberty, alone on her own island, the restored Main Hall of Ellis Island gleamed in the slanting sun.

My thoughts of the port and our claims on it were focused

on Ellis Island's far gloomier southern wing. Like nearby Governors, and so many other islands in the archipelago city, this huge section of Ellis Island remained unused and abandoned, although not entirely uncared for. Its low buildings were the hospital wards where immigrants waited and many died.

For thirty years after 1954, when the federal government abandoned it, the entire island languished in disrepair. Today the Great Hall and immigration museum are, with the Statue of Liberty, major tourist attractions, but the unrestored hospital wing remains a reminder of those whose hopes of a future in Golden America were dashed on that island.

This duality occurred to Georges Perec, the playful, enigmatic French author, when he visited Ellis Island in 1978, two years after the American bicentennial when Ellis Island was declared a national monument. Although still in ruins, the island was opened to the public for limited visits. For Perec, who wrote about it in *Ellis Island,* a small book of poems and vignettes, the island was a "place of absence, a non-place, nowhere," known throughout Europe during the thirty years of its operation as "*l'ile des larmes, isola delle lagrime,* island of tears." It was inhabited by the spirits of 16 million immigrants who had stopped there thinking they were in America but were only in a sort of bureaucratic limbo at the doorstep to America. Four-fifths of the millions who came through the Great Hall spent less than five hours on the island, but those hours could be extremely nerve-racking, especially if the initial screening interview led to a dreaded special inquiry for health or political or other reasons. Only 2 percent of the immigrants were turned back, but for the rejected it was catastrophic. Between 1892 and 1924 there were three thousand suicides on the island.

At its peak, as many as ten thousand immigrants a day streamed through the Great Hall. Perec wrote that Ellis Island "belongs to all those who were chased and are still being chased by misery and intolerance from the lands of their youth." My father's mother, Hannah, came through the immigration gates at Castle Clinton in 1884, before Ellis Island. When she told me how it felt to arrive in America, after living as a child through pogroms and discrimination, her eyes widened as if she were seeing the Manhattan skyline again for the first time.

AFTER SOME EASY PREPARATIONS in the galley, Susan and I had dinner and watched a showy sunset over the city and surrounding upper bay. We lolled on *Tradition*'s broad deck while night settled around us and Manhattan's infinite windows blazed like nearby stars. Then we climbed below for a good night's sleep in the cabin's wide and gently rocking double berth.

5 / Concrete

The hole was half a city block square, and went down over
fifty feet deep into hard rock. Pools of grayish water, high
derricks, piles of cable and twelve-by-twelve timbers, large
boulders, steam shovels, compression machines, shanties,
tool sheds and endless pipe filled the space between the
walls of jagged rock. Luigi received his brass work check
and proceeded in the line of laborers to the shanty.

—Pietro Di Donato, *Christ in Concrete*

*T*he morning after we beached our friends on the shore of Battery Park City, I hauled anchor at the earliest crack of dawn. Without raising sail, I pointed *Tradition* toward the southern tip of Governors Island across from the Battery, allowing the waning ebb tide to carry us across Anchorage Channel in the upper bay. The flood tide would begin just before sunrise, and then we would turn up Buttermilk Channel and into the East River.

Susan was still fast asleep in the cabin, deep under the covers. The engine's exhaust tapped out its regular *put-swish-put* sounds. Before making way, I'd managed to light our crotchety alcohol stove without too much clatter. I sat alone at the wheel, my reward a steaming mug of hot coffee and the dawning light over the peaks of lower Manhattan and the towers of the East River bridges. On my left in the morning gloom passed the gathering auto traffic on the East River Drive; on my right loomed the pilings and broad warehouses of Brooklyn's Red Hook shore.

We had almost six hours of favorable tide ahead of us but needed only about two hours to get *Tradition* through the difficult Hell Gate passage under the Triborough Bridge at northern Manhattan. I wanted to anchor for breakfast above the Williamsburg Bridge, near Kips Bay, on the Manhattan side of the East River. There was a place on the river I'd always wanted to show Susan from the water's edge, a spot on the Manhattan side at Twenty-First Street. In the earliest days of our courtship there was a construction yard and dock there that played a significant part in our lives.

Governors Island was shrouded in mist and shadows. I could make out only its ugliest landmark, the massive concrete ventilation tower for the Brooklyn-Battery Tunnel, but the island's remarkable ice-cream-cone shape and its truly beautiful historic structures remained hidden. Originally known as Nuttin Island, it was purchased from the Indians by the Dutch and then became the summer residence of the English governors during the colonial period. "Black Jack" Pershing departed from the island with his Expeditionary Forces when the United States entered World War I. In 1998 the Coast Guard vacated the 175-acre island, which it had used for decades as its primary East Coast base, creating the most important opportunity for new harbor development in the past century. The rounded original island, about ninety acres, has been designated a historic district, and it includes some of the most beautiful forts and early-nineteenth-century military housing anywhere in the harbor. The island's second section, a cone-shaped piece of filled land is open for development of all kinds; less than ten minutes from the Manhattan financial district by ferry, it could become a city-within-the-city, like Battery Park City and Roosevelt Island. The complication for all developers and would-be concrete contractors is that some portion of private revenues will have to subsidize the island's ferry service. It is also probable that private developers, in return for building rights in the nonhistoric area of the island, would be required to assist in the restoration and maintenance of the parks and historic buildings that will make the island a stunning but expensive addition to the public waterfront.

Tradition chugged past the tip of Governors Island and into Buttermilk Channel, which runs along its Brooklyn-facing shore. The light was still dim, but I could make out the high ground where Fort William was built two years before the War of 1812. A few of the mansions of Officers Row were also visible beyond the modern docks at water's edge. As we came closer to the island, I noticed a security vehicle cruising along a nearby road, its light flashing a warning that the island was strictly off-limits and could be visited only by prearranged tours. I thought about Senator Daniel Patrick Moynihan, who did so much to preserve the important historic and parklike areas of the island, and I wondered who the heroes of the island's future might be and whether they would want small boats to tie up anywhere on its shores. As I write this, there is intense wrangling about the island among federal, state, and local government agencies. The federal government is threatening to place the entire island on the real estate market. That would solve very little because much of the original military property is on the historic register and cannot be razed. The eventual plan for the island will undoubtedly include public and private areas. I wondered if I would live to see any of the island become open to the public. Governors is a beautiful island, but it had been off-limits to New Yorkers for most of its history.

We passed the air ventilator tower, clear of the island. Each year this stretch of the harbor gains ferry traffic of all kinds as the renaissance in waterborne commutation continues. I cut *Tradition's* wheel to head her over toward the hard shore of the financial district. We neared the Vietnam Veterans Memorial at Coenties Slip, a park that also marks the spot where a Dutch couple, dockmasters celebrated in New Amsterdam for their affectionate good humor, once moored incoming boat traffic. Coenrat Ten Eyck and his wife, Antye Ten Eycke—Coen and Antye's slip—Coenties Slip. Before chrome-and-steel office buildings took their place, the old warehouses and abandoned depots of Coenties Slip and nearby Pearl Street were home to artists like Agnes Martin, Ellsworth Kelly, Ann Wilson, James Rosenquist, Jasper Johns, and Robert Rauschenberg, people who kept New York at the center of the modern art world while being continually chased from their lofts for illegally squatting in them. Across South Street, which runs parallel to the Manhattan shore, we could clearly see Wall Street itself, which was once the walled edge of protected New Amsterdam. In the mid-1700s, during British rule and well before the street became synonymous with international capital, the East River landing at Wall Street was the site of a thriving public slave market. Here prominent New Yorkers, whose names grace numerous city streets, bought and sold human chattel. After the Revolution and the tumultuous years of debate over the Constitution, General George Washington's barge departed from Elizabethtown, New Jersey, crossed the bay and landed at the East River foot of Wall Street on April 23, 1789, for his inauguration in what was then the nation's capital.

Early morning joggers along South Street glanced up from their exercise at our catboat out in the channel. A steady and warm southwesterly hummed in my left ear. It whispered about how lazy I was not to raise the sail for tacking under the approaching bridges. But the voice of reason answered that in just a short while we would anchor for breakfast. Besides, very soon the Manhattan towers would break the flow of southwestern wind, and under the three upcoming bridges—the Brooklyn, Manhattan, and Williamsburg—the wind is always willful. Booted and slickered fishmongers piled crates of fish on the edge of the Fulton Fish Market, still one of the few active working piers on this stretch of the Manhattan shore. Here and there, in windows up in the high-rise apartment buildings, I glimpsed a human form or two amid the glare of the rising sun. From their vantage above the river, *Tradition* must have seemed insignificant. Dwarfed by the immensity of Manhattan and bobbing out on the broad East River, she would have looked like a fat wood chip forced upriver by the surging tide.

I had to shield my eyes against the rising eastern sun to see up to the high span of the Brooklyn Bridge. I always made this part of the trip with shivers of joy and some fear. The Brooklyn and her sister bridges usually displayed some hanging evidence of maintenance work: scaffolding, safety netting, rigging cables and ropes, and other swaying potential hazards. Will an errant rivet or bolt, or forgotten crescent wrench, or perhaps just a careening hubcap choose this moment to fall on our heads? Unlikely, I told myself, and nudged *Tradition*'s throttle up a bit to quickly clear the span.

Elation, awe, fear, elation: these are the usual feelings of an East River passage under the bridges between Brooklyn and lower Manhattan. It's not the same on a major sailing or motor yacht. On *Tradition* the water is about two feet away. Seaworthy but old, the boat took the East River at her own slow pace, but with the current running at almost three knots, she was probably making about seven knots over the river bottom.

Under minimal engine power, *Tradition* glided easily upriver on the incoming tide along the palisade of apartment houses at the edge of the East River, beyond the gray stacks of the 14th Street power station. Manhattan's eastern shore, from well below Fourteenth Street to Twenty-Third Street, is walled by massive blocks of apartment houses, punctuated by some well-used parks all along the shore just above the river's bulkheads. Here the river is a great moat below hundreds and hundreds of lower-income and subsidized middle-income apartments with river views and tree-lined blocks. These apartments were New York's gift to the war generation and a reminder of a time when the city pioneered the construction of affordable housing in prime locations. The dense apartment-house neighborhoods of Stuveysant Town and Peter Cooper Village are set off from the river by the humming FDR Drive. In fact, all along its short course from sound to sea, the East River, really a tidal strait since it joins two bays—moves in sympathy with the city's own endless movements. Its broad reach is spanned by throbbing bridges, clunking bridges, bridges with clattering trains, and even walking bridges. After the Brooklyn, Manhattan, and Williamsburg Bridges, the river opens into even broader and quieter reaches like Kips Bay and Turtle Bay. Beyond the Queensboro Bridge, the river builds up a chop and begins to swirl its way through the Hell Gate.

Tradition passed under the Williamsburg Bridge just as a clattering subway train passed over, headed for Brooklyn. The sun had risen over distant Queens and the city was bathed in light, while upriver on Kips Bay, well below the 59th Street Bridge, the early morning river sparkled. Just below Twenty-Third Street, I turned *Tradition* toward the Manhattan shore and slowly brought her close to the seawall at the river's edge.

With the engine in neutral, I hopped forward and dropped anchor. As I suspected, the anchor blades clunked down in about ten feet of water against a concrete bottom. I felt the anchor slide off the submerged concrete mound, bite into East River sand and silt, and then catch. I snubbed the line and came back to the cockpit to cut the engine. For untold minutes I sat listening to the gulls and whistles and mingled automotive sounds of the morning city.

ALONG THE FDR DRIVE at Twenty-Third Street there is little living evidence that this Manhattan shore was once a dockers' world and a waterfront of immense activity. After the war, when the "shape-up"—the longshoremen's early morning hiring ritual—still existed on some East River piers, the housing cliffs began to rise from the Manhattan shale. The river then was still busy with traffic of all kinds, far more so than the tugs, oil lighters, luxury yachts, and small powerboats one sees today.

In 1961 when I was mooning over Susan, a college girl living out her fantasies far away in France. The city was still in the bloom of growth after the war, and the constant parade of working tugboats plowed deep furrows in the river. That summer I was a laborer on the Transit Mix Concrete Corporation's dock, right where we anchored *Tradition*. At the river's edge, with the sun warming *Tradition*'s broad deck, I could almost see this riverfront as it was thirty years ago on a similarly languid morning: "*Listen, kid, I want you to go out and sweep the dock around the string piece out at the end. That's where the old man is coming in soon. It's gotta look good, okay?"*

The yard foreman, Vinny Boyle, sent me to the edge of the dock well beyond where the trucks would be parked at the end of the day. This assignment often came on a clear day, and I would be delighted to have the chance to loaf while seeming to work far out on the long dock, almost in the river itself. William McCormack, MR. BIG OF THE WATERFRONT as he was often called in the tabloid papers in 1959, would soon be arriving in his elegant motor yacht, and Vinny Boyle needed to see that proper preparations were made for his arrival. A black limo would be out there to greet the white-haired gentleman and his entourage, so a great deal of sweeping was unnecessary, but it was important to have a laborer cleaning up for effect. As the limo whisked away Mr. Big, I imagined his broad-shouldered chauffeur muttering to the old man, "That's Danny Kornblum's kid sweeping the string piece."

The yard and the dock were among the most active ready-mixed concrete-supply sites in the city. Its silos for construction materials towered four or five stories over the East River Drive. The dock on either side was crowded with barges carrying mountains of sand or gravel. From this dock on the East River had come a great deal of the concrete for all that good housing along the river, as well as innumerable commercial sites inside the island. The controversial Pan Am building (later MetLife) was going up then, destroying forever the beautiful expanse of Park Avenue with its silhouette of Grand Central and its lower-rise office buildings. My neighborhood friend Bill Salerno was an electrician's summer helper high up in its scaffolding, and both of us felt something of the pride that construction workers take in shaping the city's skyline. There were so many big jobs in the fifties and early sixties, including tall office buildings in lower Manhattan, near the Colonial and Transit Mix East River yards. The frenzy of building in Manhattan meant that the entire construction industry would be tied up immediately if the concrete drivers' Teamsters Local #282 went out on strike —which it did with some frequency in those days.

Honking car horns up on the FDR Drive broke my reverie, and I glanced up at a momentary traffic jam. I wondered when the last barges or tugs had put in at this spot on the river. Today the concrete industry is far more mobile than it was then; yards spring up to serve temporary needs and are then dismantled when the pouring is over. Barges can come and go in scores of different coves. There are landings aplenty along the city's 500-plus miles of shoreline, much of it now prized as potential water's edge view and background for expensive residential property. At our breakfast anchorage the lapping calm of the river's edge was relaxing and quite unexpected on a part of the waterfront I had once known to be so terribly busy in the very early morning . . .

"Hey, kid, wake up. Time to do the switch on the barges." The gruff voice from my youth belonged to Dominic, whom the truck drivers called the Seagull. A gnarled boss of the dock's laborers, the Seagull had a leather face and a proud Roman nose, and despite the fact that he stood as tall as my rib cage, he was the undisputed master of shifting the barges. After the crane had emptied the sand or stone from one of the cavernous steel barges and into the silo-shaped hoppers above our heads, it was the laborers' job to bring new, heavily laden barges into place where the crane's massive jaws could bite into the mounds of building material and lift it up from the barges.

To swing the barges into position, we looped hawsers as thick as a man's forearm around powerful winches at the dock's edge. We jumped between the dock and the barge decks, tossing a dock line over a capstan, ran down the dock to await the swinging end of a barge as it eased up against the dock, and tried all the time to second-guess the Seagull's *sotto voce* plans. "Tide and wind, tide and wind," he'd mutter. "Can't let that wind catch youse longways wit an empty barge, can't pull nuttin too good against yer wind and tide out there . . ." The tugs picked up the empties and left us another string of full barges for the coming days. Planning the moves and calculating the tides and winds was the Seagull's preoccupation. Sometimes the barges had a jerry-built shanty on one end that housed a gruff barge tender, often a couple with a scruffy dog. One or another of the barge tenders would come out and hand over a line or offer some profanity-punctuated commentary on our maneuvering. The barges seemed almost the size of an office building's floor and could be extremely unforgiving. "Be careful, kid," the Seagull would yell to me over the wind. "Yer slip off wit d'barge comin in, get yer leg crushed" . . . "Careful with d'winch, kid, that rope'll twist yerdickoff."

After the barges were eased into place, either in position for emptying at the crane or out on the pier where the empties were stationed, it was time for coffee. All phases of the day were marked by the coffee ritual.

I was the lowest among the dockworkers, so errands to the coffee stand were an important part of my job. Anyone could ask me to get them a cup and whatever else they wanted, and often they paid for mine, too. Harry the Horse had a coffee cart leaning up against the corrugated steel at the water's edge. The dock on Twentieth Street next to ours was piled high with huge rolls of newsprint in those days when there were still morning and evening papers printed in the city. The stevedores there were mostly strong black men, who normally only talked among themselves. There was not much camaraderie at the coffee cart except what Harry carried on in Manhattan wisecrack banter. The stevedores were in their thirties and older and were among the élite of the city's black working class. They made good money on the docks and liked to eat fat sandwiches. When both docks took breaks at the same time, it was chaotic in front of Harry's red coffee cart. But as the Seagull's gofer and the McCormack kid, I never had to wait or shout my order. Harry himself would peer over the crowd of broad-shouldered, sweaty black and white men and shout "Whattlitbe, kid? The usual, right? Don't gimme no bullshit—this ain't no time to play fuck around."

I had no lines in this dramatic ritual—just smile, reach for the coffees, squeeze through the waiting crowd, get the hell out of there. Around me the men would be trading news of horses or discussing the latest development in a contract negotiation or a pending strike. If I stood there for the entire lunch hour, something I rarely did, I would see hundreds of men of every description on that waterfront—all with money in their pockets and many with houses or apartments in New Jersey and the five New York boroughs. Hundreds of men, white and black working for good union wages on the waterfront. I sat along the string piece away from the jousting joking of the men, eating a sandwich and feeling the hot sun baking sore muscles.

Sometimes there would be more macabre bantering: "Hey, Ronnie, dja see d'stiff dey fished outta d'river last night?" Scabrous drunks sometimes slept off their loads in the big truck cabs. One old alcoholic couple was grudgingly tolerated, but most were chased away as the men came to claim their rigs. It was said around the string piece that the bums sometimes fell into the river, but on occasion they fought and were pushed.

At our shoreline anchorage years later, the river's flowing water looked immensely better than it did in those days. I saw no feces and no dead bodies, but very few other boats, either. Just upriver from where we were anchored was a small private marina for private yachts, mostly luxury motor jobs and charter vessels. Otherwise, at least during that time after sunrise, there wasn't much marine activity near the shore, only the occasional tug passing out in the river's main channel.

At Transit Mix the pay was premium union construction wages; at least twice as much as the minimum wage, and you had the romance of the river and its endless stories. Many of my college mates would have shied away from the backbreaking work and its lower-class associations, but I felt privileged to be in this world, doing a man's physical work. I had learned to work hard on upstate dairy farms as a summer farmhand for four years during high school. I was almost six-three, a lean 190 pounds, and my body yearned to test its strength against hard work. But physical qualifications had almost nothing to do with the fact that I was hired by the Transit Mix Concrete Corporation. It had, on the other hand, everything to do with my father's relation to Mr. Big of the New York waterfront.

"I was with one of the waterfront groups today," my father, Daniel, mentioned casually over dinner one night when I was nearing the summer of my nineteenth year and wondering what I might do for work during the long school break. "One of the McCormack guys said there might be a job open, a good laborer's job. Bill McCormack himself mentioned something about putting you on as a laborer. You need to go see the foreman of the East River plant at Twenty-First Street. They'll have something for you."

The dock strikes of the 1950s were everyday conversation in our home. My father was the city's labor mediator in those years, a commissioner. He was always involved in the labor negotiations, often for tense days at a time. If the cement drivers were out on strike, or the tug crews, or the longshoremen, the papers would fly banners about the crisis, and in the case of the waterfront strikes they would always allude to the mysterious influence of Mr. Big, whose empire spanned the rivers and bays. Although my father had cordial relations with all the waterfront characters and powers, he would never have dreamed of accepting a personal favor that might even hint of a conflict of interest. But in the summer of 1959 my dad had just "left the city," as he would say. He had begun to build a private labor law and arbitration practice.

That first predawn morning at the bus stop, I discovered the work life of people who lived in my own neighborhood whom I had never before seen: a terribly thin woman whose ankles floated in her high heels exactly like Popeye's wife Olive Oyl, chain-smoking Luckies; a crew of construction workers, most of them electricians; uncles and fathers of the Irish and Italian kids I played stickball with; and two postmen in uniforms. These bus stop regulars glanced at me in my stiff new worker's boots and jeans jacket and, unimpressed, continued breathing steam through the heat of their coffee cups.

"From the subway stop at Twenty-Third and Lex you can catch a crosstown bus to the river," I remember my father explaining with that New Yorker's special pride of mass transit mastery. "From there its a short walk to the dock." I remember climbing the steel stairs to the office perched above the bay where the trucks lined up to be filled with material. "My name is Bill Kornblum, I'm supposed to see Mr. Talon," I announced to a bored dispatcher at the grimy, coffee-stained desk overlooking the yard. "Talon ain't here," he grunted at me. "You could talk to Vinny Boyle. He's comin soon." Boyle burst into the noisy office a few minutes later, sized me up quickly, and motioned to a thin boy whom I had not noticed cowering behind his thick torso. Boyle was a handsome man, dark and well built, wearing clothes that placed him somewhere between the businessman and the construction worker. He introduced me to the cowering red-faced boy named Patrick. "You two'll work together on the labor crew," he explained. "Today I need you both to go out in the yard and fill in some of the potholes out there. You also need to smooth down the big bumps where there's concrete built up. There's shovels and a wheelbarrow ready down by the stairs. So go to it."

We worked at filling holes for three days, but Patrick began to take long breaks and finally, on the fourth day, he disappeared from the job. During the afternoon of that fourth day, Mr. Boyle came over to where I was filling the wheelbarrow and said, "Okay, kid, stash that gear. I need you to help the Seagull at the hoppers."

Boyle walked with me across the yard as I tried to figure out what help I could possibly be to a hopping seagull. We passed quickly under the truck bay, where a frenzied laborer everyone called Banana Nose stood astride the barrels of the trucks. His job was to guide a long steel chute into the proper place at the top of a mixer truck while tons of cement and other concrete-making material rushed down from the high silos above. Banana Nose always yelled at the top of his lungs, even when the noisy trucks were gone. Boyle and I crossed the blaring, white hot yard, and abruptly we were in a dark room that smelled of the bottom of the sea. My nose filled with the odor of clams, seaweed, old cigar butts . . . For a few seconds I was completely blind until my eyes became accustomed to the dim light. Gradually I could make out the shapes of three hoppers and chutes poised above a large conveyor belt and heavy levers extending from each chute. Glistening stone tumbled out of one hopper onto the belt, and the noise of the falling stone was deafening. I could make out a small man seated on a three-legged stool watching us and the falling stone alternately. The man grunted at Boyle and barely seemed to look at me. "Dom, this kid here's your helper." I said my name and shook the gnarled vise of a hand Dominick held distractedly out for me to grasp. He never asked me again for my name, and I don't think he ever called me anything but kid.

As Dominic the Seagull looked on with seeming indifference, Boyle showed me the basics of what went on in the hopper room. There were three kinds of material in the huge barges at the near end of the dock below the hoppers: stone, sand, and Lelite, the latter a volcanic-looking synthetic aggregate used to make lighter concrete for floors in high buildings. There was a panel with three lights and three bells on the wall opposite the hopper levers. When one of those signals went off, the operator simply pulled the appropriate lever and material would rush out of the silo onto the flapping conveyor belt, where it would rise a hundred feet or so up to the silos above the yard office. I began to think of those silos as the Kingdom of Banana Nose, the monarch of profanity. He pushed the buttons that ordered me to open a particular hopper chute, or in his Banana Calaban voice that seemed to arise from some deep hole in the earth, he called to me over the ancient intercom, "—grrtsumfucking sandup gggrrrthere, youfuckindeaderwhat?"

Out of about forty-five or fifty concrete drivers on that dock most were Italian and Irish. Only one was black, a loud, cantankerous man named Maxwell. He had seniority that was absolute and enforced by the driver's union delegate, a calm but authoritative veteran driver named Rocky Lofaro. The only other black man at work at the concrete dock was Bob White, a laborer who spent his days in the conveyor belt shanty perched over the FDR Drive. A tall, courtly man with gray hair, Mr. White was quiet, not a creative curser like Banana Nose or Maxwell. When he descended from his perch high above the river and down the gangway along the clacking conveyor belt, it meant that it was raining and we had to quit because the conveyor belts were slipping, or that the barge shift was about to happen and he was going to help us jockey the great barges. Whichever the message, he moved with slow grace and addressed us, even me, with Southern dignity.

Otherwise, all the men who drove the cement mixers or labored in the yard were white. Among them the taunts of Guinea, Polack, hillbilly, and so on suggested neighborhood rivalries they had carried with them from childhood, even if now they were living in New Jersey or Staten Island. The men were not a great deal like the yearning, suffering Italian immigrant proletarians in Donato's *Christ in Concrete*. They were far more American, all involved in an extremely corrupt, mob-dominated union on which their lives depended. But they were deeply connected to the profane romance of their city: the baseball, horses, the booze and the gambling. Theirs was a world of raucous male joking, sudden violence, deep laughter, and a social geography of good girls and bad girls, corruption and occasional moral clarity.

I was not too lost in thought to hear Susan stirring in the cabin. It was already after nine. She poked her head above the hatchway and yawned into the glare of the morning sun. Smiling from her rest in the gentle rocking of *Tradition*'s cabin, she came up on deck in her nightgown, oblivious to the traffic on the FDR Drive or the thousands of onlookers in the windows of Stuyvesant Town. While she took in the city, I fired up the alcohol stove and reheated the water for coffee. I passed some fruit from the cooler up to her and busied myself with some quick fried eggs and toast. The sun was warm on our faces as we sat on deck over breakfast. Drowsy from the heat despite the coffee, I felt like taking a nap while Susan went below to dress. I sprawled on the cockpit bench, my head resting on a stiff flotation pillow.

Sometimes when I was pretending to sweep the dock far out on the river I'd be joined by a group of angular Puerto Rican corner boys. With quick waves and grunts in my direction, they'd skip over the dock to dive into the water. Flotillas of raw sewage floated nearby, and sometimes they would send the smallest of their number in first to sweep away the turds with his arms: *"Hay mierda, conjo . . ."* But they were cooled while I sweated inside a concrete truck, trying to chop hardened mortar from the blades inside a barrel, my unprotected ears ringing with pain from the electric hammer's din.

I worked at Transit Mix for two summers and one fall as the Seagull's helper. Sometimes I thought I could have worked there for the rest of my life, but it was only seven or eight months of work, nothing in comparison with the Seagull's 1,080 months on the flood. And yet it was a span of time in my own life when every day and every week was filled with the intensity of youth and strength.

Dominic the gnarled, Banana Nose, Bob White the gent, Maxwell, the cement truck drivers, men in rough work clothes covering bodies of all shapes and sizes, faces unshaven until after work, grimaces with cigar butts—I could see them in my mind against the background of the new luxury condos. I wished I could talk to them and ask some of the questions a kid could never have the nerve to ask—about the mob, the loan sharks, and the raucous dice games in the drivers' locker room.

Years later a former student reintroduced me to her father, Rocky Lofaro, the Transit Mix shop steward, and I asked him about the union battles and the drivers' brushes with danger. Retired after more than thirty years of driving a concrete mixer truck in Manhattan's traffic, Lofaro had broken in as a mixer driver on the Empire State Building job: "The ramps at the foundation were steep and deep, I mean real deep." The mixer trucks had no power breaks and easily stalled. "Coming down the ramp with a full load of concrete was murder. You were ramming down on that mechanical break like your life was at stake, and it was." One of Rocky's last jobs before retiring was hauling concrete for the foundations of the World Trade Center.

Bob White, the gentlemanly black laborer who had resided in the shanty high above the FDR Drive all those years, died over the winter of 1961 while I was away at college. His lungs, the Seagull explained, in one of his longer speeches in my memory, "they just gave out on him from all the dust. Too bad 'cause he was such a nice quiet guy, a good family man, too." When I came back the next June to claim my job again, I was sent up to Bob White's post in the shanty. Each morning over the summer and fall of 1961 I climbed the catwalk along the conveyer belt to the shanty above the docks high above the river. I had the most glorious view of the East River bridges, the palisades of Stuyvesant Town and Peter Cooper Village, the endless coming and going of river traffic. Filling and refilling the three giant hoppers under my feet, pushing buttons to let the Seagull know what material to send up, watching the stones bounce and ricochet against the steel walls, or the sand thump in wet waves on the growing pile, waiting to see the material fill the hopper—these were tasks that left ample time for thought and daydreaming and, most blessed of all, for reading. This was a union job, one that came with the tacit agreement that if you did your work and there was some free time, there was no need to "look busy." Up in the shanty I was in my own world. As long as the material flowed smoothly I could read, sing, shout to the skies, stare at the river and the clouds . . . Every so often the Seagull would call me down with either the coffee sign or the signal to come help shift the barges. Otherwise, up in my shanty, I was free and alone to rant and dream.

Many times I toyed with the idea of staying on that job indefinitely, of continuing my program of reading and writing while perched above the city. At night I studied French and English literature at NYU; I was torn during the day between hoping for overtime pay and going to class. I read Melville and Shakespeare as the conveyor belt rushed sand and stone into my hoppers. Melville had wandered this waterfront and mused over the ships and longed for adventure, just as I did. Like wild Walt, he was a New Yorker a boy could admire. Somewhere I found Charles Olsen's passionate study, *Call Me Ishmael,* which traced the influences of real shipwrecks and real events on the creation of *Moby Dick.* I was inspired by Melville's visions of the sea and strange lands. I could almost feel the slippery whale blubber on the decks as I pretended to be high up in the lookout nest on the *Pequod*'s foremast.

In *Tradition*'s cockpit, breakfast was over and Susan had finished straightening up while I was lost in concrete reveries. With the sun climbing over the flashing East River, I started the engine and made ready to get under way. Susan took the wheel while I went forward to raise the anchor. Onshore, sleek BMWs and Mercedes jockeyed for position in front of waterfront condominium towers. I wondered whether, if we had stayed into the heat of the afternoon, we might have seen some kids come looking for a place to dive into the river.

With a few grunts and pulls, the anchor loosened from the ooze and submerged concrete from old Transit Mix trucks. Susan cut the wheel to head the boat away from shore. *Tradition* pointed her bow upriver toward the whimsical modernity of the 59th Street Bridge.

6 / *East River Passage*

The third basic type of soldier is less aggressive,
using its head instead to block the nest entrance—
thus serving literally as a living door. The head may
be shield shaped . . . or plug shaped.

—Edward O. Wilson, *Sociobiology*

*I*t was just after nine when Susan and I headed up the East River from the old site of the Transit Mix dock for the short but intense passage to the Hell Gate. After breakfast, we had about four hours remaining on a favorable tide. In principle that tide would take us through the Hell Gate and out past Flushing Bay and then to the Throgs Neck, the entrance to Long Island Sound. Normally, the stretch of river from Twenty-First Street to the Hell Gate at the Triborough Bridge would take far less than two hours. I relaxed with the knowledge that we would have plenty of time on the remaining hours of flood tide. We would even be able to tack back and forth across the river to study the city from every angle.

We headed *Tradition* out on the Kips Bay and Turtle Bay reaches of the East River, from about Twenty-First Street to the beginning of Roosevelt Island at the United Nations complex, around Forty-Second Street. The river is broad on this northward stretch above the Williamsburg Bridge. The wind collected force and blew the sailboat along with the tide at a good clip. We had *Tradition*'s sail up full. I cut the engine and let the wind take over from the noisy clatter. Out toward the middle of the river, away from the Manhattan canyons, the wind swept over the water from the southwest and flattened the twinkling surface. In the distance we could see some people fishing from small powerboats. They were working the tide rips at the southern end of Roosevelt Island. Sailing on a starboard tack, with the boom payed out over the boat's port combing, we headed in a direction that would bring us below the spot where Newtown Creek sends its industrial waste into the East River.

Newtown Creek divides Brooklyn from Queens, and like so many of the city's tidal fingers, it flows deep into the urban interior. More a small river than a creek, the Newtown twists through a maze of communities like Greenpoint, Long Island City, and Maspeth, and even some communities of the dead, like Calvary Cemetery buried amid sprawling industrial neighborhoods and spanned by the elevated roadways of Queens. These are the inner city necropoli that confront the people in their cars on the snarled Long Island and Brooklyn-Queens expressways.

Susan and I sometimes get into a minor dispute on this

section of the New York passage over whether to play sailors in the East River or traverse quickly to get through the Hell Gate and out to the cruising grounds of Long Island Sound. Susan generally wanted to get through the Hell Gate and be done with it. I liked to dawdle when possible and even take side excursions into the industrial creeks. While we were going through this ritual debate, Susan looked back and noticed a McAllister tug pulling a huge string of barges toward us. At one point or another on the passage there was always at least once such overtaking. But the powerful tug, running about eight or ten miles an hour, was still a quarter-mile away. We were heading east toward the Queens river shore, into shallower waters outside the main channel, and in moments we would be safely outside the tug's course. Best of all, I argued, we would be able to watch the tug pull her heavy tow past us, and I reminded Susan of the lore of tugs and how much the girls and Noah loved *Scuffy the Tugboat* when they were little. Susan rolled her eyes. Despite her bouts of big-harbor anxiety, though, I knew she too loved the feeling of being within the city yet outside it, afloat on the river.

Nearing the Brooklyn shore at Williamsburg-Greenpoint, we were met by the acrid smell of heated tar on rotted wood and rusted metal. For me it was the smell of childhood summer explorations through the tarred backwaters of oily, industrial Flushing Creek, another of the city's heavily polluted tidal rivers. I gazed up at the Greenpoint shore, at streets I had never seen. How many New Yorkers, I wondered, would know how to find India Street and its creaky piers and turn-of-the-century warehouses? Or adjacent Java and Huron Streets, which end at a massive jumble of jagged and rotting piers and blackened pilings? We came up on that ghostly corner of commerce quickly as we approached the extreme northwestern corner of Brooklyn at the mouth of Newtown Creek.

On the end of a huge and apparently unused warehouse along the dock at Huron Street, an immense painted sign read: HUXLEY ENVELOPES. BUY AMERICAN. Under it a smaller graffiti scrawl marked a visit from the Greenpoint Untouchable Gang. This corner of Brooklyn's Greenpoint harks back to a time when these streets were not just dead ends at a decrepit industrial riverbank. Newtown Creek was the main thoroughfare for Dutch and English settlers in Maspeth. In colonial times, John Waldman wrote in *Heartbeats in the Muck*, large ships could sail four miles up Newtown Creek into a lagoon near Maspeth Heights. Above the lagoon, along Maspeth Marsh, the wealthy owned summer homes where they fished and hunted in the early 1800s. Throughout most of the nineteenth century, the creek was one of the busiest shipping channels in the nation, but the marshes were poisoned by sludge acids. Much of the creek's length was lined with cargo barges. Small streets like India and Huron ended at long docks, where sailing vessels and then steamships sat before heading out to seaports over distant oceans. The area was an important ironmaking and shipbuilding center of the port by the time of the Civil War. The Union's first steel warship, the *Monitor*, the famous "cheesebox on a raft," was built there. By the late nineteenth century, Newtown Creek was the site of the city's first major oil port, featuring primitive refineries that loaded the creek bed with layers of benthic pollutants. By the early decades of the twentieth century, the creek had gained a reputation, along with the Gowanus Canal in Brooklyn, as a reeking and infectious sump. "In September 1891," Waldman noted, "members of the Fifteenth Ward Smelling Committee embarked on a voyage up the creek to determine the sources of foul odors that permeated their streets. The air became riper as they passed cargo ships, manure scows, a dog pound, and sausage factories where they saw heaps of flesh rotting in open doorways." When they arrived at the oil refineries, they reported that "'the stenches began asserting themselves with all the vigor of fully developed stenches.'" By the early decades of the twentieth century, over 5.6 million tons of cargo were shipped in and out of Newtown Creek, more than the total shipped along the entire Mississippi River. From *Tradition* the creek seemed quiet, with no barge traffic at all. But Newtown Creek is no ghost port. Near the shore we could see a trailer truck backing into yawning warehouse doors and workers inside waving directions.

Coming too fast too soon upon the submerged piers at India Street, we spilled wind to let the strong river current carry us along the shore toward the creek's gloomy gray mouth. Here the shore was lined with gasoline storage centers, massive red brick factories and warehouses, some vacant, some filled with new entrepreneurial and artistic energy. The old factories and warehouses, attractive as lofts for artists or start-up businesses, loomed along the waterway and blocked our wind. There were hundreds of industrial lofts in Greenpoint, many inhabited by young artists who, like their predecessors on the Manhattan waterfront, were constantly being chased from illegal conversions of industrial lofts into residences. And like Red Hook and so many other old riverfront communities of the city, Greenpoint was cruelly bisected by a Moses-era highway on stilts, the infamous Brooklyn-Queens Expressway.

The tide was pushing us up into the river, but to maintain helm I turned on the engine, with an apologetic shrug in Susan's direction. A bit frustrated with me, but always game to explore, Susan welcomed the engine but not our course, away from the big river and into the industrial tributary. Only a few moments, I assured her. We would go up Newtown Creek only for a short exploration.

We could see places on the shore where the seawall was badly eroded. Nature, in the form of grassy tufts and sandy outcroppings, was reclaiming her shoreline. We saw no real evidence of the creek's old maritime culture, no barges, no tugs, just the rotted seawall and occasional bollards or cleats to hint at the area's riverine past. Barges still make their way up to some of the modern oil and gasoline storage and transfer yards, and to a few other industrial chemical plants along the creek, but we saw none that day. With some encouragement, a colorful neighborhood of houseboats could flourish in the creek: prime and quiet waterfront, within reach of subways and buses, ideal for the kind of barge and houseboat neighborhood one finds in Seattle's Lake Union or along the Seine in Paris or the Thames in London. Houseboat dwellers in New York are tucked here and there in the big creeks or isolated on piers across the Hudson in Jersey, and a few live year-round on boats at Manhattan's West 79th Street Boat Basin, but they often have a difficult time with unsympathetic authorities. I had a momentary fantasy of finding a berth for *Tradition* at a bulkhead along this antiquated but still dramatic industrial waterfront. Then we reached the arch of the Kosciusko Bridge, which carries the Brooklyn-Queens Expressway over the Newtown Creek's industrial mazes, and, as I had promised Susan, we turned to head back out on the powerful East River flood tide.

It's not a good idea to come up too close to those black and jagged remnants of the old port on either side of the shore at Newtown Creek. There's danger from submerged pilings, so we tacked away from Brooklyn and Queens and faced the broad and vertical expanse of Manhattan.

The rubble that was once Transit Mix and the piers around Twenty-First Street appeared as a distant white pile under the deep reds of the massive Peter Stuyvesant and Peter Cooper housing complexes, themselves horizontally bisected by the arching FDR Drive and divided at Fourteenth Street by a huge red electrical plant, its four gray stacks a thumbless hand barring invasion from the water. Along the river, above Twenty-Third Street, the new complexes of riverfront condos hid a far larger phalanx of minor and major skyscrapers, including all the world-class towers of midtown. As we neared the middle reach of the river, *Tradition*'s sail filled with a steadying breeze. She heeled just enough to set her mast against the Manhattan skyline at a slightly rakish angle. We glided effortlessly with the wind against an immovable backdrop of concrete giants.

Poring over our nautical chart, Susan noticed the lack of proper names for most of Manhattan's streets and avenues. Fifth Avenue, Park, Madison, Thirty-Fourth and Forty-Second Streets—almost none of the prime real estate was named, not even Trump City or Trump Towers. I pointed out that a few landmark buildings, like the Empire State and the Chrysler, were named on the chart, but Susan was more impressed with how the nautical perspective levels the high and mighty. Even famous buildings by the most acclaimed architects are anonymous. Bellevue is just "hospital" on the chart. What counts, she realized, is that it's big and could be a hospital and that's what you see from the river. The Empire State and Chrysler buildings are named because they stand out as landmarks any sailor would recognize.

We spent a few more moments that morning pondering the East River section of the standard nautical chart while the boat sailed steadily toward the Manhattan shore at about Thirty-Fourth Street. We were on a direct course for the Empire State Building and for the renovated Altman's building that now houses the Graduate Center of City University. We failed to find my office on the chart. Instead we found the important data· river depths, buoy positions and characteristics, the danger of old wrecks, conditions of the river bottom from an anchor's perspective, the vertical heights of bridge spans. These were the important details on the nautical charts. No hyperbole distracts the mariner.

The East River tide, now running at over four knots, took us quickly past Thirty-Fourth Street and up into the low Forties. It swept us toward the line of rocky shoals that extend southward from the point of Roosevelt Island, where earlier we had seen the fishermen. But the wind picked up, steady from the southwest, and I hauled in on the sheet to pinch upwind and slow our uptown, upriver progress. We could sail beautifully in this wide stretch of the river. *Tradition* pointed her bow almost directly for East Forty-Second Street and the United Nations. There was plenty of water, at least five hundred yards, between us and the Manhattan shore, and we were still far from the green buoy at mid-river. Under us was about thirty feet of East River water. And below the river bottom, with sonar, we might have heard the subterranean tunnel traffic, cars and trains rushing through tubes buried under the mud and rock.

Aside from the steady passage of cars on the FDR Drive and the traffic along the streets, there were few striking signs of human activity in midtown Manhattan. It's a strange feeling to see the towering city from the East River or the Hudson and not be able to discern people, to know that at the cross streets inside, the island's multitudes await the Walk signs at the crosswalks, commuters duck into the subway stations and line up at the bus stops, crowds jostle on the sidewalks. With binoculars, one can see office workers in the buildings busy on their phones, people in shirtsleeves entering and leaving rooms, and the occasional dentist staring into an open mouth. With only the naked eye the nearby city is distant, people are contained in their cars, buses, and buildings.

Manhattan Island is broad and convex at Forty-Second Street. It curves up from the East River and turns down somewhat past Fifth Avenue, where it disappears into Times Square and the edge of the Hudson. The wind that reached us from Forty-Second Street and surrounding smaller streets carried the occasional faint zoo smells of urine and fermenting garbage and the odors of internal combustion. And then the cell phone rang.

Our friend Phil was calling from our home in Long Beach, where he and his fiancée, Jackie, were staying for the weekend and taking care of our dogs in the bargain. Their news was not good. Jackie's favorite aunt was suddenly quite ill. Her cancer had been in remission for months, but she was being admitted to Sloan-Kettering that afternoon. I braced myself for the complications faced by the urban cruiser who is away and not away. Jackie's family in Harlem needed her to come quickly for a bedside vigil at the hospital. Phil suggested that he could bring the dogs along to the hospital in our ancient, nine-passenger Chevy Caprice station wagon. They could stay in the back, and he would come out to the parking lot and walk them at intervals. He insisted that this was a good plan. Susan and I vetoed it in favor of another. We could easily make it on the flood tide to Hallets Cove near the Queens side of the Triborough Bridge.

On their way to Harlem, Phil and Jackie could meet us at the Astoria shore, where we would take the dogs aboard. If all went well, we would still have almost two hours of favorable tide to take us through the Hell Gate and out to the sound.

So it was decided. It would take our friends about an hour to drive from Long Beach and less than that time for *Tradition* to motor along with the strong East River tide to the cove at the beginning of the Hell Gate passage. In the meantime we would continue our riverine wandering, but now with gnawing concerns about Jackie, traffic on the unpredictable Van Wyck Expressway, and where we would tie up at Hallets Cove.

I tried hard to think about the 59th Street Bridge now spanning the sky ahead. In minutes we would be passing under it and sailing past the massive public housing apartment blocks of the Queensbridge Houses. Whenever I pass the city's large public housing complexes, I think of people I have known who have lived in them and the life experiences they have had in those dense neighborhoods. The Queensbridge Houses reminded me of my former graduate student Martha Andujar, who raised her family there, including a daughter who graduated from an Ivy League university with honors while Martha worked and went to the public university and finally completed her own doctoral degree. Thinking of Martha made the high-rise apartment blocks seem far less cold and distant. I wondered where she was in that city of a billion windows . . .

Directly across from the United Nations, at about Forty-Fifth Street, a series of strong gusts pushed us directly toward

U Thant Island, or what used to be called Man-o'-War Reef. The small fishing boats that had been working the tide rips there earlier were now gone. From the boat we could easily see the silver memorial to peace and spirituality dedicated to the work and memory of former secretary general U Thant of Burma (now Myanmar). This somewhat defiant pile of rock just below the southern point of Roosevelt Island always reminds me of E. B. White. When the U.N. was conceived and organized, first in San Francisco and then at Lake Success on Long Island, White wrote a series of passionate but understated articles in *The New Yorker,* later collected in a slim and largely forgotten volume entitled *The Wild Flag.* My father read us these pieces at the dinner table. White argued that if the U.N. needed a flag at all, which he doubted since flags were too well associated with blood and battlefields, it ought to choose a cattail or a wildflower, something wild and hardy, that would push through barren earth and thrive with only fitful irrigation. Just at the foot of one of the reefs below the island, I thought I saw some cattails waving in the wind, although they might have been wild young sumac trees. The hope of world government still clings to a foothold on this Manhattan shore.

I headed *Tradition* east of Roosevelt Island. The Queens passage under the Queensboro Bridge was calmer but lacked the spectacular architectural sweep of the passing Manhattan skyline. The Manhattan passage was often a more exciting ride due to a set of standing waves, sometimes as high as three to four feet, which might extend for almost half a mile along the river between the East River Drive and Roosevelt Island. Captain Prime, my sometime mentor and fellow catboat lover, once explained to me why this chute of waves occurred. "It's a narrow channel in the East River with the strong current," he said. "If a tug runs through with its high power and big wake, the swell they throw goes out on each side and hits the shore. The waves bounce back so you have a cross sea, and that's something else to be careful about. It's not really dangerous, just uncomfortable."

The reward in this section of the river is the passage under the Queensboro Bridge at Fifty-Ninth Street. Its industrial Gothic towers built of girders and crossed steel beams sliver the sunlight, and each tower is topped with a sort of steel bonnet, inspired, one might almost imagine, by Tenniel's Red Queen. All these details became more visible with each minute as *Tradition* bobbed along the tide toward the bridge itself.

For my Brooklynite parents, the bridge of bridges was Roebling's Brooklyn. The New York City bridge of *my* dreams was the Queensboro Bridge, as it must have been for Paul Simon, another Queens boy, who wrote it a love song. I remember venturing out of the sickly green classrooms of ancient P.S. 22 and crossing the Queensboro into the city on a chattering school bus bound for the Museum of Natural History. The phantasmagorical shapes of its steel girders, always distorted by the crossing shadows of more girders, appeared in my dreams. There was an elevator on the bridge at mid-span, just off the main roadway, where lonely-looking men waited to descend far below to the island in the river. Sometimes the bus would stop for unknown reasons in mid-span, and we would be suspended over the river while clutching our lunch boxes.

From the Queens channel of the river, looking up from *Tradition*'s cockpit at the water's surface, Roosevelt Island (formerly Welfare Island, and before that Blackwell's) looked like a pilot fish alongside Manhattan's higher spines. The island is dominated by banks of condo apartments with fabulous views of the bridges and urban canyons, but its lower-cost apartments add income diversity to the community, which has its own esplanade on either river shore. By all accounts, life on the island combines some of the benefits of the urban village where neighbors can be known with the endless variety of Manhattan still just a subway or tram ride away. We motored close to the island's Queens shore, the sail now hanging slack in the largely windless midtown gorge. Trees and occasional green shrubs clung to the stonework on the island's forbidding seawalls.

Like almost all the city's smaller islands, Roosevelt was once a place of exile and isolation. The city authorities purchased it from the Blackwell family in 1828 for a new prison, with plans for the subsequent construction there of the city's almshouse, its madhouse, and eventually its first island hospital for infectious diseases. Charles Dickens visited Blackwell's on his trip to the United States in 1842 and was sickened by the living conditions of its inmates. In the next century Mae West was imprisoned for ten days in the island's penitentiary on obscenity charges after the play she coauthored and starred in, *Sex,* was closed by the censors and authorities. The pioneering muckraking journalist Nelly Bly wrote *Ten Days in a Madhouse,* a famous and grimly detailed denunciation of conditions in the mental wards in 1887. And in the 1920s the La Guardia administration exposed conditions in the island's prison where jailed Tammany political crooks and regular racketeers and gangsters were living it up on smuggled whiskey, food, drugs, and other luxuries. The prison was closed and the inmates moved to the new Rikers Island prison facility on the other side of the Hell Gate passage. The insane were moved as well, to Ward's Island under the Triborough Bridge in the Hell Gate section beyond Roosevelt Island. Then called Welfare Island, Roosevelt Island remained a center for the physical isolation and treatment of patients with smallpox, TB, venereal diseases, and other infectious or socially deviant maladies. Eventually most of those hospitals were closed or moved elsewhere, and the island was converted into a residential community.

THERE WAS SO MUCH to see on the East River and so many new angles to see it from that the speed of the current and the additional speed of the engine were a mixed blessing. I would have liked the time to let my eyes linger: on the geometric shapes of the Queensboro Bridge and the vaults underneath where a fancy market was installed; on the gondola of the Roosevelt Island tramway swaying against strong cables; on the old Manhattan tenements that persist here and there amid the banks of East Side luxury apartments; on the medical cliffs of New York Hospital; on the traffic on the Drive. But all passed by in movie time, each giving way too soon to the next attraction.

On the Queens shore the neighborhoods moved past in the same slow motion. Blocks of public housing mingled with older frame dwellings and even older factories and warehouses. We were reaching the limits of Long Island City and beginning to motor-sail along Astoria's riverfront. Our destination was not far ahead.

Lowering sail generally required putting the boat's nose directly into the wind so the sail would hang slack and within easy reach. With her face in the wind, *Tradition* thrashed about in the river swells. Fickle gusts from all directions made it difficult for Susan to know where to hold *Tradition*'s bow.

The heavy gaff, a fifteen-foot round spar atop the sail, helped speed the sail downward, as did the boat's rolling motion. After years of hoisting *Tradition*'s sail up and easing it down, I almost had it down to a science. Almost. As the gaff was lowering at its throat, along the mast, one of the wooden mast hoops caught in the gaff jaws. The sail, gaff, and attendant rigging stuck in place and would not descend no matter what oath or spell I cast. There was nothing to do but hoist sail up aways, allow the stuck mast hoop to slide down first, and then resume lowering the gaff to its position parallel to the boom. Two forty-foot sailboats, their sails furled and under smooth diesel power, glided past on their way through the approaching Hell Gate. Susan set in the boom crutch, a wooden plank that fit into a slot to the rear of the wheel and held the boom and sail above our heads when it wasn't aloft in the wind. Just as we had secured the heavy boom in its crutch, a large plastic cabin cruiser churned up a monster wake thirty yards from us. Its steep waves rolled us about and threatened to smash me against the spars as I gathered the sail that was nested in the lazy jacks. These light lines run on either side of a gaff-rigged sail and prevent the unfurled cloth from dipping into the water or otherwise covering the crew swaying in the cockpit, trying to furl the sail.

Susan continued heading the boat toward our next buoy marker while I tied in the sail stops. Sometimes I would find myself hanging on the boom, my arms wrapped around spar and sail, as the boat dipped and rolled. We were specks out on the river while on both sides of us, everywhere just out of our sight, was a city of people.

Sailors on the East River approaching the Hell Gate from the south mark the miniature Gothic lighthouse that stands in a park at the northern end of Roosevelt Island. Here the river widens out again to the left, and Hallets Point is directly east of the island's tip and its lighthouse.

The point is part of the vibrant Astoria community, home to some of the city's larger Greek, Slavic, and Italian-American populations, another aging blue-collar community with a growing number of recent arrivals. It is connected to Manhattan by a short subway ride, so it's become a place of refuge for the young and educated who are being squeezed out of the center by the older and wealthier.

Hallets Cove was a tranquil spot and refuge, a rare designated anchorage in a busy part of the river near the Hell Gate, away from the tugs and major power cruisers that churn waters. I had never put in there before. Captain Prime had told me about its charms. Our chart showed that near the shore the depth went from fifty to thirteen feet, and possibly less: a shallow place to wade ashore. Below the cove itself, on a modest promontory, was Socrates Sculpture Park, the creation of artists and community activists. The park was directly at the water's edge, framed at its mainland border by a huge, largely vacant red brick factory building. On the southern edge of the park was a sculpture studio and a number of artists working on their pieces.

Two hundred yards or so from the shore, we could already make out some of the larger pieces of art, their surprising shapes flouting conventional scale. Here and there amid the sculptures, couples and dog walkers and small groups of art appreciators strolled along the shore with spectacular views of Manhattan and the river. The park itself I knew well, but only from the land. I was not sure where to try to get close to the shore and anchor. Almost all the East River banks were heavily built up and forbidding, and even after careful examination of the chart I was at a loss as to how we might make our dog pickup.

"Where exactly," Susan asked, "do you propose to do this landing?"

"Do you see Phil and Jackie yet?" I countered. "I bet they're just getting on the Grand Central Parkway. We have time to find a suitable spot. Then we'll anchor and pump up the dinghy." Susan seemed unconvinced.

The current was still moving us along steadily, but it slackened quickly as we edged toward land. The shoreline remained unfamiliar. By my calculations Phil and Jackie and the dogs were probably at least twenty minutes away. The current was much reduced, and we had *Tradition* running at just above idle speed as we cruised along the river's edge looking for a suitable landing spot. We dared not approach closer than about fifty yards, but that was close enough to see the shoreline more clearly. This was one of those many times I wished that *Tradition*'s old depth finder was still working, but its signal had been silent for years. We had become used to having a boat hook to figure out the depth where we ran aground. But we didn't want to run aground in the East River, which would mean a likely collision with an ancient dock piling or cement slab with rebar daggers through the hull, not just a bump on a friendly sandbar.

I coaxed *Tradition* toward a promising spot on the shore just at the edge of Socrates Park. From our vantage it looked like a small indentation, probably not a cove, but perhaps a congenial spot for going ashore. We slowly approached the water's edge. Just ahead of us, I could see we were about to smash into a set of teacups, each about eight inches in diameter, poised on equally out-of-scale saucers and barring entry. Some of this china was almost submerged in the river; other pieces stood on thin rods of various heights elevated above the water. To the left of this whimsical shoreline tea setting, our course was menaced by the jagged beams of a ruined segment of industrial dock. Next to these black pier hulks rose a great cubic formation of whitewashed peat moss bales that marked the end of what I had hoped was an inviting landing spot. We immediately recognized the hulking peat formation as Knut Wold's Peat Moss sculpture, which we had seen in the park a few weeks earlier; the semisubmerged teacups were Elisa Proctor's *Sustenance*. Rather than become a boat mired in an aquatic china shop or risk sticking our bowsprit in a bale of peat moss, we turned *Tradition* away from the shoals of art to seek a genuine landing somewhere onshore.

I followed the shore northeast past one gloomy and wrecked industrial property, well decorated with razor wire but with no accessible shoreline, and then another. Then, beyond the industrial wastes, we spied a small cove with no evident obstructions, industrial or artistic, to prevent our approach. And as we did approach the shore we found to our delight and surprise that there was an actual beach at the water's edge. To call fifty feet of sand a beach is perhaps an exaggeration, but for us it was an amazing sight. Behind the beach a small park sloped down to the water. This was Hallets Cove Park, one of the rare soft landings along the entire waterway system of inner-city New York. Susan took over the wheel and backed *Tradition* to a stop. The current, in the protection of the small cove, was almost still. I went forward to set the anchor, which disappeared into about ten feet of water. The weak current moved the boat against the anchor line, and soon its flukes had set themselves well into the welcoming sand.

"Make sure it's secure," Susan warned. "I don't want to be floating around out here with you and the dogs onshore." I let out extra line and backed the boat against the anchor. The anchor held fast. I went below to wrestle with the dinghy, a deflated rubber mass just aft of the mast step in the forward area of the cabin. With much grunting and only one small head bump, I hoisted the dinghy out onto *Tradition*'s cabin house deck and began the process of assembling it for our landing.

Tradition's dinghy is itself a vessel worthy of brief comment. It is a small, inflatable craft, neither a toy nor a chubby inflatable Avon or Zodiac dinghy that must be pulled along in the water. It's called a Caligari Gigi, of Italian origin, and one of the earliest models of an inflatable boat: about six feet long and almost three feet wide when inflated, with a collapsible wooden keel and floorboards. It has oarlocks and is capable of taking a small outboard. We bought it for a hundred dollars from a dyspeptic elderly man in Rego Park, Queens, who said his son had once dreamed of owning a larger boat and had purchased the dinghy as a starter. We used it for about eight years with great success. If it ever developed a leak, which it did from time to time, it was easily fixed with a conventional bicycle tire tube patch kit. Susan liked to call it the *Gigi,* and she pretended the word means "dinghy" in Italian. ("Okay, Cap'n, go pump up your *Gigi.*") But sometimes she called it "the Dinghy of Dr. Caligari." Whatever one calls it, I was making quick work with the foot pump and the dinghy was almost ready to launch when Susan called out, "There they are, up on the road."

I looked up to see Phil waving from the window of our battered station wagon. I could see the dogs jumping over the backseat. The dinghy splashed into the East River, and I flopped into it with only the least bit of rolling around and looking ridiculous. Over my shoulder as I rowed, I saw Phil and Jackie and the dogs walking down the grass slope to meet me at the shore. Daisy, our fifteen-year-old cockapoo, was picking her way along the sand. Young Bosun, the Labrador, was making dashes into the water, all the while barking at me to hurry up and get to the shore. It was about one in the afternoon, but there was not another soul in the small beach park. My friends stood calmly waiting for my arrival while the dogs went off sniffing in different directions.

I hopped out and pulled the dinghy up on the sand while Bosun did leaps and bounds around me and Daisy grunted in my direction, already anticipating shivering in the hated dinghy. But Bo couldn't wait to get going. He hopped into the Gigi even before I had a chance to greet our friends.

They waved and blew kisses to Susan out on *Tradition,* while I gathered the dogs in the dinghy and shoved off into the gray waters of the East River.

"Stay in the boat, Bo," I ordered in my best dog-master voice. He has the annoying habit of hanging over the bow, ready to dive in the water any second. Daisy cowered under my legs, making it difficult to row the dinghy. We were more than halfway to where *Tradition* was anchored when, trying to move Daisy out of my way, I jerked the dinghy and Bo pitched forward into the river. He came paddling around the dinghy, a powerful web-footed swimmer, surprised but happy to be in the water. I cursed and swung the dinghy in his direction. As he came alongside I grabbed the harness Phil had remembered to put on him at home. With his front paws over the side and me pulling on the harness, he was back in the dinghy in a second. My relief was brief. Dripping water, Bo circled about in the small boat and then shook himself so that I was treated, full in the face, to a drenching East River shower.

We hoisted the wet dogs up on *Tradition* with no great trouble. Our friends on shore waved one last time and were gone on their way up to the Triborough Bridge and on to Harlem. Susan settled the dogs while I deflated and stowed the dinghy. In a matter of minutes we were ready to up anchor. I gunned the engine, which protested at the demand, and we headed into the current toward the Triborough Bridge and its sister, the Hell Gate railroad bridge, spanning the Bronx and Queens.

7 / *The Hell Gate*

Resignedly beneath the sky
   the melancholy waters lie.
So blend the turrets and shadows there
That all seem pendulous in air,
While from a proud tower in the town
   death looks gigantically down.

            —Edgar Allan Poe, "The City in the Sea"

No es sueño la vida. Alerta! Alerta! Alerta!
Nos caemos de las escaleras para comer la tierra humeda.

            —Federico García Lorca, *Poet in New York*

*I*n a few minutes the welcoming Hallets Cove beach was a dash of sand in the distance. The massive whitewashed cube of peat moss at nearby Socrates Park became a faint landmark. Across the river, on the Manhattan shore, were Harlem's red brick apartments and housing projects, and on 116th and Pleasant Avenue, just at the river's shore, I could easily make out the cavernous shape of the old Ben Franklin High School where I had worked years before. In the distance, Manhattan Island rose gently uphill toward Morningside Heights, Columbia, and City College. In about one hour the tide would turn against us as millions of gallons of Long Island Sound water shouldered its way downriver. But the passage wouldn't take nearly that long. A warm front was coming, no doubt, for the temperature was rising and oppressive humidity had begun to settle in along with the low, dirty flannel clouds that are an August specialty in New York. In the gloom of cloudy weather, moving toward late summer dusk and twilight, the passage was filled with dark memories and forebodings. Hell Gate is a graveyard for ships and sailors and passengers, its islands the refuge of the wayward and unwanted.

The Dutch called it Helegat, or Bright Passage. At the turn of the twentieth century, once some of its worst obstacles had been removed, an article in *Harper's* described the passage in bucolic terms:

> There are boat-houses at the water's edge, and trim little cat-boats and sloops are moored to private wharves. Straggling little canals lead off into the sedge, which ripples in the wind; and along here, toward five o'clock in the afternoon, is a sight which cannot be seen anywhere in the world. Between the low banks, and towering above them come the steamers which connect at New London, Stonington, Providence, and Fall River with the railway for Boston, their colors streaming, and the passengers promenading to the music of their string bands."

Even today, the passage can be extremely bright after a storm front passes and sunlight plays on the water and glints off the bridges and roadway guardrails. But as *Tradition* chugged along in the gathering tide, we headed into a squishy low front of heat and humidity. There were no sandy banks or marshes along the shore, and the air smelled faintly of garbage and jet fuel.

We plunged directly into the middle of the river. The wary small-craft captain might think it wise to hug the shore and remain out of the main traffic channels in these swift currents of five knots or more. Captain Prime had taught me that this was not always a good idea when rounding Hallets Point because of the way the currents eddy around the Astoria shore. When you get to Pot Cove on the northern end of Hallets Point in Astoria, the tugs may fool you, I remember him explaining.

Just for the fun of things when we came up with a tug, sometimes running light [with no loaded barges] against the current, we'd come right along the shore because out here when you reach this spot the tide swirls around and runs the other way along the shore and so you hit this spot and all of a sudden you are in fair tide, so you may see some daredevil coming around the corner at Hallets Point.

I wanted to give *Tradition* plenty of time to get out of the way of oncoming tug traffic. Another friend, Michael Kortchmar, boatbuilder and former captain of the sloop *Pioneer* out of the South Street Seaport, advised monitoring channel 13 for bridge-to-bridge traffic. "Hail the approaching ship on the radio," Michael advises, "and make sure the helmsperson sees you." I mentally practiced the laconic style of American men who know they have the right stuff and speak on their radios like Chuck Yeager.

Small whirlpools appeared before *Tradition*'s bow, not dangerous but enough to swing her around. I fought the wheel to keep her on course. *Tradition*'s ancient rack-and-pinion steering had a bit too much play in it. She needed to be swung in one direction and then the other, in a series of ever smaller turns of the wheel. The Hell Gate's strong and erratic currents were a challenge. Fortunately, traffic that afternoon in the passage was extremely light. The current rushed us past stone embankments and a precious stretch of parkland along Randalls Island and then closer to the Triborough Bridge and the drab concrete cliffs of the Wards Island mental hospitals, towering many stories over the bridge roadway.

EARLY EXPLORERS LIKE Adriaen Block clawed their way through the boiling tide rips and rockbound rapids of the Hell Gate under the power of sail and fear. They kept ship's lifeboats, anchors, and grappling hooks always at the ready. For most of two colonial centuries, commercial river pilots and captains learned to negotiate the passage and gradually the various hazards took on familiar names of respect and gallows humor. The passage was a nautical obstacle course. Raging waters from the Harlem and East Rivers eddied around Pot Rock, Greater and Little Mill Rocks, Hen and Chickens, Frying Pan, Negro Head, Bald Headed Billy, Bread and Cheese, the Hog's Back,

Flood Rock Island, and others. Local fishermen in the mid-nineteenth century fished all over the port, and rowing skiff rental places thrived in many spots along the shores. No fishing spot was more popular than the rapids of the Hell Gate, noted for some of the region's very best striped bass fishing. Fishermen dared the edges of the rapids while during the same period about a thousand commercial ships struck the dangerous shoals. A Hell Gate passage was essential to reach the many ports of Westchester, Long Island, and Connecticut, and saved hours on the trip to Boston or New York through the calmer waters of Long Island Sound. But a great deal of commercial shipping preferred to take the slower ocean route into New York Harbor. By the mid-nineteenth century, the U.S. Army was obsessed with making the Hell Gate passage less dangerous.

Starting in 1851 and continuing for the next seventy years, the army blasted the submerged ledges and dangerous surface rocks. Those explosions were some of the young nation's earliest and most spectacular earthmoving projects. They would be dwarfed eventually by the earthmoving exploits of railroad and then interstate highway construction, and by the atomic obliteration of Japanese cities and entire Pacific atolls, but at the time they were big events. The largest occurred in 1885 when, before an appreciative crowd of thousands who lined the riverbanks, the formidable nine-acre expanse of Flood Rock was blasted into history by tons of carefully set army explosives. Reports claim the shock of the blast was felt as far away as Princeton, New Jersey, well beyond the Hudson. The *New York Times* devoted its entire cover page to the event and interpreted it smugly as another triumph of human will over nature.

WITH THE EXCEPTION of Mill Rock, where kayakers routinely rest and wait for a favorable tide to carry them up the Harlem River, the old obstacles are now entirely purged from the Hell Gate. Even so, as I fought her swinging wheel and struggled to keep her yawing to a minimum, we were reminded why the Hell Gate remains an anxious passage for a small boat like *Tradition*. The Hell Gate passage itself ends just beyond the Triborough Bridge. Beyond that some nasty tide rips and strong currents guard the Bronx and Queens shores. I relaxed a bit when we got there, for *Tradition* always has a way of calming the tide rips. She moved swiftly along with the strong current. A red-and-black Moran tug hauling strings of construction barges passed us quickly and at a comfortable distance in the favorable current.

Then everything changed for the worse. I noticed white smoke rising over *Tradition*'s stern. A wave of panic rose in my chest. There was no reassuring sound of water splashing out of the exhaust. Invariably that signaled a water pump problem, most likely a shredded impeller inside the pump. The engine was overheating. In seconds it could have become a lump of scrap steel. I cut the ignition to shut the engine, and we drifted without power at the mercy of the Hell Gate currents.

I barked at Susan to take the wheel while I hurried to raise sail. We had not bothered to do so earlier since the winds were light that afternoon and were always extremely fickle on that walled stretch of the river. I scurried along the deck to remove the sail ties, then jumped back into the cockpit and hauled on both halyards as fast as I could to get the sail aloft. The hauling left me breathless and drenched with sweat. With no wind the sail flapped to no effect. The current carried us clear of the railroad bridge along a most ugly stretch of the Bronx's Morrisania shore, where sludge barges loaded up at one of the city's main sewage treatment plants. On our right, at a distance, we approached the forbidding profile of Rikers Island with its blocks of prisons and razor-wire fences and the innumerable gray buildings of the largest prison-city in the nation.

It was a straight shot downriver from the arch of the Hell Gate railroad bridge to North and South Brother Islands. We needed to get out of the main channel and into shallower water, where we could either anchor or tie up somewhere. I remembered the ruins of a pier and a ferry dock on the Bronx side of the abandoned North Brother Island. Perhaps we could find a puff of wind to help steer us with the favorable current into a safe haven for repairs.

The current died just as we were passing the Sunken Meadows section of Randalls Island. The marshy Bronx Kill and the industrial Stony Point section of the Bronx's Port Morris were almost dead abeam. But I was no longer watching the sights. The water became smooth and dark, still. Slack tide. Quickly *Tradition* lost her forward way, and with no wind we sat in the river going nowhere. I raised the engine box and saw immediately that we had broken the belt that turns the water pump. There could also have been a problem inside the pump, for all I could tell. We had little more than half an hour of slack tide before the current would begin taking us back downriver, to who-knew-what precarious landing. I knew I needed more than that to do the repairs. There was no wind. Here and there through the low clouds a hazy August sun beat down on *Tradition*'s wooden decks. We were hot, sweaty, and nervous. I hated the idea of trying to anchor in unprotected water, but it might be necessary if the tide turned against us.

After a while a few puffs of wind did reach *Tradition*'s hanging sail and pushed us some yards closer to North Brother Island. I began to have some hope. The wind died, and the boat meandered closer to the Bronx shore and a phalanx of smelly sludge barges. We had a full view of the razor-wire shores of Rikers Island over on the other side of the river. Things went on this way for a while. Errant puffs of wind moved us closer to North Brother Island and then died. We wondered if we could anchor or tie up on the island before the ebbing current began moving us backward. With twenty minutes before the tide shifted, Susan began lobbying for a radio call to the commercial towing service for help getting to our destination just four or five miles downriver, at the mouth of the Long Island Sound. But I wanted none of that ignominy and expense. We ought to be able to extricate ourselves from this jam, I pleaded. So we waited.

Finally, a few sustained puffs of wind sent *Tradition* heading easily along the western shore of North Brother Island. We found the jagged bulkheads of the defunct ferry docks, rounded into the wind, and eased against a set of wooden pilings near the dock's edge. With some dispute and confusion we managed to secure the boat. Now the dogs awoke and clamored to go ashore. Susan gave them water and settled them down again. She then went with them below, in a silent snit, to stay out of the sun. I collected my wits and tools and hunched over the engine box. Fortunately I had a spare belt and a spare pump impeller.

Repairs that day came rather easily. I remember dropping only one or two screws into the bilge water. It took me forty minutes to complete the job and have the engine running well again, although it continued to cough a bit through its fouled carburetor, as it had before the breakdown. By then, though, the current had set against us. I watched in frustration as the flowing water pulled *Tradition*'s dock lines taut, in a downtown direction. The engine would not be powerful enough to make headway against the opposing current. Susan was fast asleep in the cooler dark of the cabin. The dogs alongside her were sleeping blissfully as *Tradition* rose and fell on the river's gentle swells. It was by then almost five in the afternoon, and the tide would not turn again until about 9:30 P.M. Night was not a problem. We could easily pick our way in the dark, following the large, flashing buoys that mark the proper channels past Flushing Bay and toward the Whitestone and Throgs Neck Bridges. No one was waiting for us to come home and we had no plans of our own, except that it had hardly been our intention to stay out into the middle of the night. Waves of heat shimmered along the industrial Bronx shore. Gulls shrieked crossly at us before disappearing behind the desolate ruins of North Brother Island's abandoned isolation hospital, former home of Mary Mallon, a.k.a. Typhoid Mary, and the dying ground of mothers and children from the *General Slocum*.

The burning of the *General Slocum* is an epic of the Hell Gate. Banner headlines across the *New York Times* edition of June 16, 1904, screamed the tragic details:

1,000 LIVES MAY BE LOST IN BURNING OF
THE EXCURSION BOAT GEN. SLOCUM

St. Mark's Church Excursion Ends in Disaster in East River
Close to Land and Safety.

---

693 BODIES FOUND—HUNDREDS MISSING OR INJURED

Flames Following Explosion Drive Scores to Death in the Water.

FIERCE STRUGGLES FOR ROTTEN LIFE PRESERVERS

The Captain, Instead of Making for the Nearest Landing,
Runs the Doomed Vessel Ashore on North Brother Island in
Deep Water—Many Thrilling Rescues—Few Men on Board
to Stem the Panic of Women and Children.

Strictly speaking, the disaster was not at all due to conditions in the Hell Gate. The *General Slocum* was an excursion ferry built in 1891 with a rated capacity of three thousand passengers. On June 15, 1904, the ferry was chartered by St. Mark's Lutheran Church in the East Village. Some 1,358 members of Kleindeutschland (Little Germany), the tightly knit German immigrant community then surrounding Tompkins Square on the Lower East Side, boarded the ferry around nine that morning at a pier on Third Street and the East River. They were bound for an annual picnic at Locust Point in bucolic Huntington on Long Island's North Shore. Their beloved pastor, Reverend George Haas, and leaders of the church were with them on deck. The *Times* reported that the *General Slocum,* which had been recently overhauled, departed with much fanfare that morning. "As she cast off and stood out into the stream her flags were flying, the band was playing a lively air, and her three decks were crowded to their capacity with a happy throng that looked for a pleasant day's outing at Locust Point, on the Sound." The majority of passengers were women and children.

The captain was William van Schaick, sixty-eight years old and commander of a crew of twenty-three men. He had earlier been cited for having ferried millions of passengers with an unblemished safety record.

Just as the *General Slocum* was passing Sunken Meadow, adjacent to Randalls Island in the Hell Gate, almost under where the Triborough Bridge spans the river today, cries of "Fire!" broke out below. "It was only a matter of seconds until the entire forward part of the boat was a mass of flames," the *Times* reporters continued, and passengers began rushing madly over the three decks to avoid the flames, "All this time full speed ahead was maintained, and the flames, fanned fiercely by the wind, ate their way swiftly toward the hapless women and babies that were crowded on all the decks astern." The skipper looked out from his pilothouse and saw "a fierce blaze—the wildest I have ever seen."

I started to head for One Hundred and Thirty-fourth Street, but was warned off by the captain of a tugboat, who shouted to me that the boat would set fire to the lumber yards and oil tanks there. Besides I knew that the shore was lined with rocks and the boat would founder if I put in there. I then fixed upon North Brother Island.

With fire raging completely out of control and decks already collapsing on terror-struck women and children, Captain Van Schaick, his own clothes on fire, stayed at the wheel and ran the *Slocum* up on the shore of the hospital island beyond the Hell Gate, but in a part of the river where the current remained extremely swift. As the captain remembered it, "I stuck to my post in the pilothouse until my cap caught fire. We were then about twenty-five feet off North Brother Island. She went on the beach, bow on, in about twenty-five feet of water. . . . Most of the people aft, where the fire raged fiercest, jumped in when we were in deep water, and were carried away. We had no chance to lower the lifeboats. They were burned before the crew could get at them."

North Brother Island became a scene of courage and panic. City Health Commissioner Darlington happened to be on the island that day, visiting the hospital. "I will never be able to forget the scene, the utter horror of it," he said. "The patients in the contagious wards, especially in the scarlet fever ward, went wild at things they saw from their windows and went screaming and beating at the doors until it took fifty nurses and doctors to quiet them. They were all locked up. Along the beach the boats were carrying in the living and dying and towing in the dead."

All told, 1,021 perished out of the original 1,358 who boarded the ship that morning. But there were miracles. One little boy was thrown into the river in midstream clutching his stuffed toy dog. He was fished from the river unharmed, still clutching the prized dog. Tales of heroism and cruelty filled the newspaper accounts for days and weeks after the event. A heroic captain ran his tug alongside the *General Slocum* in full exposure to the fire and saved over a hundred lives. A measles patient from the island hospital ran into the water despite her fever and saved a few children. A nurse who always wished she could swim ran into the river to grab some children, which she did again and again until she was swept into deeper water, where she discovered that she *could* swim and continued saving lives. Others were antiheros. Crowds of souvenir hunters made collecting bodies difficult in the ensuing days. There were some ghoulish stories of onlookers who stripped bodies of their jewelry. And over and again bystanders described the unconscionable behavior of a private captain who was said to have watched the horror from the safety of a great white motor yacht without ever lifting a finger or launching a boat to assist in the rescues. "Kept His Yacht Back While Scores Perished: White Vessel's Captain Watched *Slocum* Horror Through Glasses," the *Times* headline stated.

Still burning at its waterline, the *General Slocum* was carried off in the current for another thousand yards or so until it struck land at Hunts Point in the Bronx. It remained there, a burnt and partially sunken hull, for the next few weeks. Divers searched for bodies in its sunken remains. Police and rescue parties combed the riverbanks for miles in search of bodies. The *Times* reported that on the night of June 14, 1904, "grief-crazed crowds" lined the shore where the bodies were being brought in by the boat-load: "Scores were prevented from throwing themselves into the river." Terrible weeks of recrimination, accusation, investigation, and trials followed the disaster. There were reports of rotten life jackets and fire hoses that burst under pressure. Some jackets were found to have been stuffed with metal to give them the regulation weight. The captain and crew were pilloried in the press, as were the ship's owners. Captain Van Schaick was sentenced to ten years in prison for his part in the disaster but was pardoned four years later by President Taft. Kleindeutchland never recovered. The German settlement moved uptown to what was known as Yorkville, on the East Side overlooking the site of the disaster, and to Astoria in Queens. The burning of the *General Slocum* remains one of the worst disasters in New York City history.

THE BUILDING OF THE prison-city on Rikers Island in the early thirties, during the depths of the Depression, was made even gloomier by a lesser-known marine disaster: the explosion and sinking of the steamship *Observation*. It was originally built in 1888, but despite her tired condition the steamer ferried hundreds of construction workers back and forth between Rikers and Port Morris in the Bronx. As she was pulling within a few boat lengths of her berth on a fair and clear morning, September 9, 1932, the ship's boiler exploded. A cement-company lighter, the *Gypsum*, was moored astern of the *Observation*'s intended berth. In the vessel's pilothouse the *Gypsum*'s captain was changing his clothes. "I had turned for a moment," he told a *New York Times* reporter, "to get a pair of trousers when the exlosion came. All I could see was a cloud of dust and smoke. When that cleared away, there was no *Observation* left, only wreckage." Construction workers and sailors were thrown far into the air, most killed instantly. The search for the dead and missing took some days and was complicated by the death and disappearance of the ship's fare collector and the death of the captain. In the end, the police determined that 72 people out of 127 on board that day perished. Most of the casualties were ironworkers, staunch union members of the Bridge, Structural, and Ornamental Ironworkers Association, as were my mother's brothers, my ironworker uncles, although they never worked on Rikers or anywhere on that tormented stretch of the river.

I REACHED FOR OUR charts and the tide tables, making sure for the sixth time that I had read the tides correctly, and confirmed that it would indeed be about six hours before we could resume our course to the sound's entrance. As I mused over the charts, I caught the flashing light of a speeding police boat. It raced toward us from the direction of Rikers and approached our temporary resting place. Two New York City cops, their faces partially hidden behind dark sunglasses, were standing at the controls. As they approached, one of them spoke into his hailer: "MOVE OUT. THERE IS NO ANCHORING OR DOCKING ALLOWED ON THE ISLAND. MOVE OUT." I tried to answer over the noise of their motor. We had no hailer on *Tradition,* but I shouted as loud as I could. They seemed not to hear my faltering explanation that we were only tied up for repairs. "MOVE ON, NOW. YOU ARE IN ILLEGAL WATER. THIS ISLAND IS OFF-LIMITS." I tried again to make myself understood. The dogs had awakened and were barking at the police boat. I could see the two officers scowl and wave their arms to shoo us away. Susan stumbled up on deck, rubbing sleep out of her eyes. She pointed to the engine box and held up a wrench. Then she held up the tide book. The police boat came closer. The officers could easily see that there were only the two of us and the dogs aboard. The sight of a woman seemed to change their demeanor for the better. Susan shouted that we were only waiting for the next tide so we could continue heading east. Then came a final blast from their hailer: "BE OUT OF HERE ON THE NEXT TIDE OR YOU WILL BE TAKEN IN." Then they roared off again.

"Who the hell wants to be here in the first place?" Susan said. "This is one spooky island."

She didn't know the half of it, as I hadn't told her the story of the *General Slocum*. But even with no historical background to conjure tormented spirits, the screeches of gulls and the black cormorants stretching their wings in the broken windows of the island's ruins made this one of the most fearsome-looking places in the city. Susan was heartened by the news that our engine was fixed, though. Together we made some sandwiches and shared a cold drink from the cooler below. The hazy late afternoon sun was descending over the Triborough Bridge and the South Bronx shores, and I could see the summer traffic slowing to a stop. Our situation was the boating equivalent of being stuck along the side of a sun-baked highway, cursing into an overheated engine. On the water the heat was oppressive. Rivulets of sweat ran down my neck. My hat was drenched from my mechanical exertions. We had hours to wait for the tide to turn. It was August 15, our thirty-second wedding anniversary.

"Well, happy anniversary, ducky," I said, with as much cheer as I could fake. Susan was not about to be either friendly or ducky, yet plainly there was some softening around the edges of her anger. "Right," she muttered. "I'm going to celebrate with a good read in the cabin." She and the dogs resumed their sprawl on the wide bunk. Alone on deck, I listened to the screech of birds from the ruined windows of the old contagious-disease hospital. From far across the river on Flushing Bay, came the intermittent roar of planes taking off and landing at La Guardia.

I needed to do something to get my mind off the gloomy late-afternoon shadows falling across the gaping ruins. In the fifties, before the buildings fell into ruin, the island had been used as a drug rehabilitation center. There were stories about kids sneaking ashore in rowboats to see girlfriends. Then I thought about these old typhoid grounds becoming a bird sanctuary, and the likelihood that the city's birders would be successful in their efforts to protect the uninhabited Brother islands, North and South, as part of a chain of bird-nesting islands in the city's river system. In a clump of marshland at the island's edge I noticed a squat night heron coming out of the shadows to pick along the shore. A flight of cormorants descended on a broken strand of riprap not far from the heron. The cormorants stretched their black wings against the drying wind, as if to ward off the curious passerby. Far above my head and farther into the island, gulls and crows careened through the vacant windows of the ruins and disappeared into the darkness. Suddenly drowsy, I stretched out on one of *Tradition*'s long benches, my head cradled on a flotation cushion, and fell into a fitful sleep.

Each time I dozed off, I was awakened by dreams or thoughts of crime and violence, inspired no doubt by the Rikers prisons across the river and the dark ruins of North Brother Island. I kept picturing young men and women I had known over the years who had been caught in the drug world and had fought addictions. Some of them had spent time on Rikers, but more had been helped over their crisis by youth programs and drug rehabilitation. In one of my dream fragments, I was standing alongside roaring water pouring over a dam. Shapes that I thought were salmon were jumping over concrete steps alongside the cataract, many falling back in exhausted failure. Later I dreamed that I was on the darkened shore of North Brother Island. The only other visible shapes were the prison blocks on Rikers. *Tradition* was nowhere to be seen. My heart beat as if it would explode.

"Yo, Bill. It's time to go."

Susan was poking my shoulder. Bosun licked my face. Without looking at Susan, I turned the key in the ignition and the engine started immediately. Our running lights and cabin light surrounded the boat in a warm glow and we untied our lines. In the gloom, the outline of the ruined North Brother hospital seemed to be leaning over us, about to fall. Across the river the lights of Rikers Island twinkled with an illusory warmth. Then in an instant we were headed into the dark and swiftly ebbing waters of the East River.

Across from Rikers on the Bronx shore, we passed a dark prison barge the size of an apartment house, moored as if waiting to catch the criminal effluent. Incoming jets curled off toward La Guardia deep into Flushing Bay. When they passed overhead, their roar was deafening. I looked across the water to the shore of College Point on the Queens side of the river and wished we could stop for a cold beer in Behan's Tavern on the shore, but I doubted that the old haunt of my Flushing youth would still be there. *Tradition* coughed and limped along steadily, and I could see beyond her bow a line of flashing buoy markers disappearing into the distance. Above them arched the roadway lights of the Whitestone Bridge, and beyond were the lights of the Throgs Neck Bridge, where we would tie up finally at the dock by my mother's apartment house and pile into a car for the forty-five-minute ride back to Long Beach.

8 / *At the Throgs Neck*

> How like the prodigal doth she return
> With over-weathered ribs and ragged sails
> Lean, rent, and beggered by the strumpet wind
>
> — *The Merchant of Venice*

> Sometimes old people snap back into life for a
> streak and start making plans, ridiculous, you know,
> when they will suddenly think of death again
> and they will see their coffins plunge upward
> like whales out of the refused depths of their minds.
>
> — A.R. Ammons, *Garbage*

*H*ello, Bill. I'm looking out the window at the boat. It looks fine. I woke up in the middle of the night dreaming about it. I dreamed it was sinking."

I interpreted that phone conversation with Martha, my mother, on a number of levels. On its surface I read it to mean that I had better get *Tradition* away from her waterfront and out of her concerned line of sight. There were pressing reasons to do this, anyway. The space satellites were tracking the first tropical storm of the season as it swirled up the coast, gathering strength.

At the Throgs Neck Bridge, the East River opens out into the first reaches of Long Island Sound. The best conventional cruising in the city and the region begins there and extends for scores of miles out the sound along the Bronx, Westchester, and Connecticut shores on the north, and along the many coves of Long Island on the south. City Island in the Bronx boasts subway access to Manhattan and points elsewhere in the city, and this marshy island of boatyards, condos, old private homes, clam bars, and spaghetti joints remains one the most popular sailing harbors for city people. Directly across the sound from City Island is the first of the glacial indentations that form the spines of fishlike Paumonok. To the east of the Throgs Neck Bridge, Fort Totten guards the entrance to peaceful Little Neck Bay and the harbors of Douglaston and Bayside, where there are thriving marinas. A forty-minute slalom ride over the parkways from South Shore Long Island brought me to Little Neck Bay and my mother's building, in the densely populated apartment section of Beechhurst at the foot of the bridge.

My plan, unformed but developing, was to get some work done on the engine and to do some sailing in the sound with friends, and then in mid-September sail back through the city to Long Beach. Nature would dash those plans.

With the storm on its way north, Susan and I knew we had to act fast and sail the boat home if possible. Our own children were either out of town or unavailable to help for the moment. We called Phil and his son Joel, a strapping lad of thirty and a professional chef in the city. Always game, they gladly joined us for a gusty afternoon and early evening on *Tradition*. We sailed under the bridge and out into the sound past Execution Rocks,

where at low tide the English in colonial times chained con-
demned prisoners to the exposed rocks to await an agonizing
death. *Tradition*'s engine got weaker with each whitecap she
parted. Aside from her chronic carburetor troubles, the shaft
and prop were fouled with marine life. A side effect of having
cleaner waters in the harbor is the more rapid growth of all
kinds of marine life on boat bottoms and prop shafts. But with
clear skies and a steady wind from the west-southwest, we
could let sail carry us. It felt liberating to be out of the narrower
river channels in the broad sound. We made long tacks across
the wind from Long Island to Westchester before we gave in
and anchored for the evening in Little Neck Bay, the first major
cove to the east of my mother's apartment building at Cryder
Point. We stopped just adjacent to the public marina at Bayside,
where streams of cars sped by on the Cross Island Parkway and
clusters of in-line skaters swayed along the shoreside path.

When we came in that evening, there was no one who could
assign us a vacant mooring. I needed a temporary mooring, despite the rather steep daily fee, if we were to have any assurance
of making it through a tropical blow in a day or so. But there
was no mooring to be had that night. Instead, we chose a spot
at the edge of the mooring field that would give us room away
from other boats. We put two anchors out with lots of extra
line, and I resolved to return the next day to secure a mooring
against the oncoming weather.

But early that next day, as I was working at home, Susan's
mother, Minerva, appeared at our back door and called for

help. Widowed for about five years, Minerva lived only two blocks from our home and was a frequent and welcome visitor. That day she looked frightened and awful. She complained of shortness of breath and extreme weakness. Susan was off on an errand. I hurried with Minerva to the Long Beach Hospital emergency room, where the triage nurse immediately sent her in to see the doctors. I waited outside and phoned Susan, who came immediately. A doctor said Minerva had "fluid on her lungs." We were sure it was a chest infection, perhaps bronchitis or, worse yet, pneumonia. But we were wrong. She had a form of rapidly growing lung cancer. The next three weeks went by in a blur of oncologists, thoracic specialists, heroic nurses, family descending at the airports, and the frenzy of impending loss.

One day after Minerva was hospitalized, the worrisome Atlantic hurricane was downgraded to a tropical storm and then to a tropical disturbance. I knew that I had to get to Bayside and find a mooring, but Minerva's illness was just being diagnosed. It was impossible to do much else but help with the more immediate crisis. The storm blew through one night, weaker than anticipated but with heavy rains and wind gusts up to sixty miles an hour. I sweated through a night of worry. Noah had just come home from medical school for a brief vacation, and the two of us rushed to the North Shore the first chance we had after the storm.

We could see from the Cross Island Parkway that *Tradition* had slipped her anchorage. She was lying far closer than I remembered to the harsh stone riprap at the edge of Fort Totten's shore. But from the distance she looked fine, although perhaps a bit low in the water. We set up the Gigi and rowed out to the boat. We discovered immediately that the pumps had failed. She had water almost up to her bunks. We were fortunate that the anchors had finally held, or the boat would have been dashed to pieces against the nearby rocks. As it was, we had lost the lovely name board that our friends Miriam and Gary had made for her many years earlier.

Noah and I quickly got the pump working again and dried out the cabin. We brought up the anchors and, with some difficulty, got the engine going. The carburetor wheezed, and the motor strained against the accumulated barnacles on the prop and shaft and began to overheat. We'd have to dive under the boat and scrape marine life from the shaft, and we'd have to make repairs on the carburetor, all before we could make the return voyage to Long Beach. And when would we do all that now, with Minerva sick? The cooperative folks at the Bayside Marina rented us a vacant mooring. We charged up the boat's two large marine batteries and left for Long Beach.

Over the next three weeks, Susan's mother's life slipped away before our eyes. We were entirely caught up in long days of illness and good-byes. There was a day or two of false hopes, but much of the time was spent in bedside vigils of tears and laughter. Susan's sisters and their families camped with us in Long Beach as they often do in the summer, but this time under far different circumstances. True to her belief that the worst sin was to be a bother to anyone else, Minverva closed her beautiful, laughing eyes for the last time surrounded by her entire family. A number of us who felt able to do so spoke at the funeral. I talked about Minerva as "the American kid" in her large family, many of whom had been born in the old country. She was the baseball fan, the party girl, the loving wife and doting mother. Susan's father had died only a few years before. Minerva believed she would join him after death somehow. I read this from Emily Dickinson to speed her weightless flight:

> Two butterflies went out at noon
>
> And waltzed above a stream,
> Then stepped straight through the firmament
> And rested on a beam;
>
> And then together bore away
> Upon a shining sea,—
> Though never yet, in any port
> Their coming mentioned be.
>
> If spoken by the distant bird,
> If met in either sea
> By frigate or my merchantman,
> Report was not to me.

My mother took Minerva's death quite hard. They had never been very close; in fact, Martha had always been somewhat jealous of Minerva's proximity to our family and her closer, more intimate relationshps with our children. But over more than thirty years these issues had faded. More recently they were friendly and loved comparing notes about grandchildren. Now my mother would be the only remaining grandparent, and she felt even more isolated and lonely. Having *Tradition* in her nearby cove during the crisis of Minerva's illness and death brought me to see her more often than usual, and she thanked the boat for that.

MARTHA HAD ALWAYS BEEN an enabler of fantasies, especially her own and those of her sons. I owe my love of boats and romantic adventure to her. Whatever interest we showed as young boys, whatever hint of precosity, my mother reinforced with immediate lessons. When I expressed an interest in sailing at the age of ten while on a family vacation in Maine, she took me to meet two old salts in Boothbay Harbor who offered sailing lessons in a beautiful open-decked catboat. Those hours spent tacking through the Boothbay moorings imprinted on me a love of New England catboats.

When my father was alive, he followed a rather narrow set of interests that included labor law, golf, baseball, and current events. He liked routine and avoided change. Despite his protests, Martha bought and restored an old country house and garden in Dover Plains, New York. She sometimes traveled alone because he was too busy to accompany her and too set in his routines to enjoy travel adventures. One summer in her late sixties she went to Ireland and even stayed for a week with crofters on the Aran Islands. She wanted to make sure she had a chance to get a long look at the country that inspired so much of the literature she loved.

She fired us with a love for literature; some of our finest family hours were spent with the four of us silently reading together. During the war she had produced a popular radio show called *Author Meets the Critics,* but she was bumped from that job by returning servicemen. My brother Pete and I knew only the barest facts about the three girl babies who had died after childbirth, depriving her of the daughters she craved. In the 1950s, after my brother's birth, she went to graduate school and became a teacher of English at Queens College of the City University of New York, where she worked for about twenty-four years.

ONE DAY ABOUT TEN years before we anchored *Tradition* in her cove and weathered the tropical storm, long after she'd retired from teaching and almost ten years after my father's death, Martha and I took a drive across the bridge to City Island. We often did that on sunny days. We strolled the main street and looked at shops, and then stopped at one of the restaurants for "a piece of fish." On our way home we ran into a sizable traffic jam at the bridge tolls. I nosed the car over to the extreme right lane, where there was a view into a boatyard. Off in the weedy section of the yard, there was the unmistakable form of a large catboat. Some of its planks were sprung, and its paint was flaking in the sun. Since the traffic was going nowhere, we pulled on to the service road and I drove into the boatyard. My mother was already dozing off in the car. I did not wake her to come with me and look at the old boat.

When I climbed onto the old catboat, I was amazed to see that the builder's plaque on its hatch beam was the modest disk of the Osterville Crosby yards. On approaching closer, I was even more amazed to see that the builder was none other than Wilton Crosby, who had also built *Tradition* in 1910. Of course, "Uncle Will Crosby" had built hundreds of catboats in his day, but most were long gone. What were the odds of my running into another of his creations here in the Bronx? I took this as some kind of omen.

The boat was close to becoming firewood or humus. Its shape seemed intact, but most other aspects were bleak. There was much rotten and semi-rotten wood topside, and major structural problems below. But conceptually at least, in its form, this was a stunning catboat. Her cockpit was immense, easily able to accommodate a small square-dance party, and the cabin was larger than *Tradition*'s.

I went to the yard office to make further inquiries. The marina owner was gruff and unsympathetic. He told me in no uncertain terms that these old boats were hazards on the water and that this one had already sunk at least once. Would he give me the name of the owner so that I might learn more about the boat's history? Not possible. That was not how it was done. I could leave a note for the owner, and if he was interested in talking to me he might call me back. I did this, and Martha and I resumed our outing.

In those days I had a research project that took me with some frequency to a public school on White Plains Road in the Bronx and therefore over the Throgs Neck Bridge. I stopped a few times at the yard just to see if there were any further developments, improvements to the boat, signs from her owner, anything. A year went by. I learned nothing further about the boat and heard no word from its owner. I was not especially aggressive about it because it was frightening to think about taking on another catboat. But there came a day after another outing to City Island, when my mother accompanied me to the yard office. As I was talking to the same gruff owner, she walked outside, around to the rear of the office shed, and found the man's wife. The two of them talked. I had the same frustrating exchange with the husband and went to collect my mother for the ride home. In the car she passed me the name and telephone number of the catboat's owner. "He's a retired tug captain," she explained. "The boat has been sitting there for a while. The captain's wife would like him to get it off their hands. You're not interested in taking that project on, are you?"

Was I? How could I be? We already had an old Crosby catboat to nurse along. But that was the issue. It was clear by then that *Tradition* was becoming weak and punky. How much longer could we count on her? She was not a good candidate for another restoration job, or so it seemed to me. If we restored this larger one, we could do more cruising with it—and with even more people aboard. Was I nuts? Was there any doubt?

The idea of taking on another old catboat never quit gnawing at me. I called the owner, who turned out to be none other than Captain Hubert S. Prime, retired tug captain and New York City harbor pilot. He *was* interested in discussing the fate of his boat, named the *Victor*. Originally built in 1916, she had been used mainly as a party fishing boat on Martha's Vineyard during the first half of the century. The live fish wells took on seawater through the hull to keep fish alive until the boat returned to port. Somehow the *Victor* had made her way to the New York area in the 1960s, before Captain Prime got her.

There is a stunning full-page photo of the *Victor* in my dog-eared and puppy-chewed copy of *The Catboat Book*. She is sailing under full reefs past Fort Totten, Queens, with her owner at the helm. I showed Susan the photo and took her along with my mother to visit the hulk in her weedy resting place. Susan remembers thinking: "Well, he has a lot of different fantasies and projects. How should I know if this is a real possibility? We'll have to get some expert advice." When I asked her nine years later why she went along with the project, she remembered thinking that we both work hard and had some money coming in. The kids' colleges were under control. And if it took a long time to get done, well, it would just take time. Susan figured that out of every ten ideas, fantasies, or schemes that I hatch, only one comes to fruition.

My mother also took a pragmatic view of the project. She knew we had paid very little for *Tradition* and had all derived immense pleasure from her for years. The money we would spend was a problem to her, but that wasn't something she would ever allow to stand in the way of a good adventure. Life was too short, she believed, to let money rule one's behavior.

"Call the boatbuilder," Susan urged me one night as I continued to pitch my boat fantasies. "Let's get an estimate so we know what's involved." We had just seen a silly baseball movie about realizing fantastic dreams, and nothing seemed out of the question.

I located boat restoration specialists on Staten Island, Kortchmar and Willner, and called them. One of the partners, Andy Willner, now a American Littoral Society baykeeper in the New York harbor, came to survey the vessel along with Captain Prime. A few days later, Susan and I drove to the Kortchmar and Willner shop to discuss the survey and building plans. I could not believe we were doing this, nor could Susan. Andy Willner gave us a rundown on the boat, saying it needed a total rebuild. His estimate of how much money it would cost was ridiculously low. He held out to us just the kind of foolish hope one yearns for at a time like that. Susan and I were immediately captivated by Michael Kortchmar, the other partner, who radiated confidence and skill and had a great sense of humor. We held our breath and told them to get a hauler to bring the boat to their yard. Captain Prime was willing to give me the boat for the symbolic one dollar if we agreed to "restore her properly," which meant in *wood,* not just by slapping on a layer of fiberglass. And so Susan and I became the owners of two Wilton Crosby wooden catboats with a combined age of 152 years.

For the next nine years, all the while voyaging through the city on *Tradition*, we worked on restoring the *Victor*. Every time we had a bit of extra money not earmarked for education or home repairs or taxes, we sent it to Michael. In that halting manner, work got done on the *Victor*. First keel scarfs and all new oak frames, then planks, and on and on. Friends with skill, particularly former machinist Bob Schrank, and friends with muscle, like Jules and Phil, helped me and Noah with some of the less skilled boat work. But for the nine years the project required, Michael and master carpenter Tom Wells carefully planned and executed every beautiful inch of the restoration.

In the meantime we kept sailing on *Tradition*, and so I began to be persuaded that I had achieved my dream: to make the boat part of our family life, not something Susan, Eve, Johanna, and my mother merely tolerated.

"What will you do with *Tradition* when the new boat is finished?" For some years in the restoration process that question needed no answer. We were still very much involved in sailing *Tradition*, and who knew if we would ever actually see the *Victor* in the water again? As the years went by and the *Victor* came back to life, the reality of owning two Crosby catboats became a more insistent problem. Noah could not bear the thought of parting with *Tradition*. Whenever he was at home and we did some work together on either *Tradition* or the *Victor*, he would lobby for keeping both boats. I dismissed this as the advice of a young man who had not yet paid the yard bills on one boat, to say nothing of maintaining a home and family.

But ever the fantasist, I did harbor thoughts of keeping both boats when the time came.

One day, a year before Minerva's death and the tropical storm that caught *Tradition* in Little Neck Bay, we received this letter from Maine:

Nov. 23, 1995

Dear Mr. and Mrs. Kornblum:

I had been in contact with the wooden boat publication and the Catboat Association to learn the whereabouts of *Tradition*. She was the first boat my father owned and our favorite. I make my living at sea and enjoy building and restoring wooden boats as a hobby.

If you could please drop me a line and let me know how she is doing. Where do you keep her in both summer and winter? I will be on Long Island in late February and would like to see her if possible. Perhaps I could provide some information regarding her history that you would find valuable.

Sincerely,

Jim Booth

Bucksport, ME

Mr. Booth's letter set off a round of speculation in my family. Was he old? Did he remember *Tradition* earlier in the century? Was ours in fact the same boat he remembered? I answered immediately. I described her lines and her history as well as I knew it, and assured him about her condition: "She stays in the water all year round. She is covered with shrink-wrap plastic from December to April and otherwise is fully commissioned for fishing, sailing, cruising, and running aground." I described her fixed keel and other faults, as well as her virtues for a young family. I explained how punky some of her decking was and, with ample warnings, implied that if she was the boat he sought, she could be his for the asking.

Jim Booth answered that he and his family just happened to be going on a vacation and would be seeing family in the New York area. Would it be possible for them to pay the boat a visit? We were delighted with the idea. The visit was soon arranged. Mid-February and bitter cold, the boat was asleep at the yard under its protective plastic covering. Jim and his family stopped at our house on a Sunday morning for coffee and bagels, and then we went to look at *Tradition*. We sat shivering in her cockpit, under a plastic cover while Jim marveled at the boat of his childhood and we told him stories of our adventures with her.

A YEAR LATER, with *Tradition* taking on water in Little Neck Bay, many work and family obligations, and another catboat to think about far out on Long Island, I was in something of a jam. There was no possibility of taking *Tradition* back through the city and around Breezy Point to Long Beach because her engine was too weak. I had run out of time, and out of available friends with time. Back in Long Beach my boatyard had closed. Howard Sacken had finally gone out of business and was temporarily living at his defunct yard. My slip was paid for through the fall, but the boat was on the other side of the city. In a real sense, *Tradition* was homeless. I made inquiries around Little Neck Bay and located a highly recommended yard in Port Washington, in the next major cove to the east. Susan, Phil, and I coaxed the old scow over there, to White's Marine at the edge of the harbor complex in the port. Mr. Joe White and his father had once run a boatyard at the top of Manhattan, and there was nothing he didn't know about boats and marinas. We were welcome to stay through the winter.

That winter we put an ad in the magazines to sell *Tradition*. We would have given her away to anyone who demonstrated a willingness to care for her, but we thought that by suggesting a price slightly lower than what we had originally paid, we just might find her a new owner. Work on the *Victor* was entering its final stages. Michael Kortchmar promised a launching the next summer. Susan urged me to contact Jim Booth up in Maine to see if he wanted *Tradition,* but something made me hesitate. Perhaps he would feel pressured. He already owned one boat and did not seem to have the time for another, despite his boyhood attachment to it. I let months go by during which I only had one or two calls about *Tradition,* none of them serious. Then I received another letter from Jim. He had read that *Tradition* was for sale and wanted to know if we would consider selling the boat to him. We were delighted; here was a genuine catboater's solution to our problems. We continued our correspondence, often interrupted by Jim's overseas assignments as a marine engineer on oil rigs. Our agreement was the usual one among boat restoration people: he would send me a dollar for the sale, and we would deal with logistical arrangements later. After a week or so I received two 1910 silver half-dollars, coined the year of *Tradition*'s launching.

On a warm fall day in 1998 a group of close friends gathered at White's Marina in Port Washington to help prepare *Tradition* for her long trip to Maine. For hours we hauled gear out of all the corners and shelves inside and outside the boat. We emptied years of careless stowage: tools, matches, life preservers, canned goods, fishing rigs, old spark plugs, out-of-date tide charts, and a few bottles of spirits. Despite its compact lines and cramped quarters, it was astounding how the detritus of everyday life seeped into the corners of a boat. The station wagon was soon filled with an embarrassing and smelly assortment of marine yard-sale items.

The boat I was giving Jim Booth—the spars, the line, the engine—was jury-rigged to an amazing degree but not very different from the boat Noah and I had found in Southold seventeen years before. Each thing we removed reminded me of the years we had kept her going and all the different ways we had abused her. We stowed all the running gear that the Booths would need to sail *Tradition* and set the spars aside for loading onto the truck to Maine.

On our lunch break in a waterfront park next to White's Marina, we sat eating deli sandwiches like a group of schoolboys enjoying an afternoon holiday from school. We sprawled at the bay's edge, enjoying the warm sand on our feet and losing ourselves to daydreams. After we ate, we drifted back to the boatyard to check on the progress at the travel lift. We discovered old *Tradition* out of the water, hoisted up on the lift's powerful slings. Exposed after so long to the fresh air, her bottom boasted a collection of sealife to make an aquarium curator jealous. Seen from a rare angle, below her ample bilges, her stubby mast actually seemed tall. Her curvaceous whale shape caught my breath, as did the sheer and the sweep of her stern, the grace of a boat that had taken us safely over the city's waters for seventeen years. I went under her hull for the last time, tapping here and there on the tough fiberglass coating over the old planking. The place where years ago Noah and I had sweated over the major repair job on the massive "deadwood" of the keel resounded to my knocking with a reassuring solid sound.

Even now, a few years since that afternoon, I imagine *Tradition* carrying on. The Booths keep her in a local yard near their home in Castine, Maine. And in due time, no doubt, Jim and his sons will get to work on her, keeping her going as a family catboat, a cruiser of home waters.

Epilogue

*F*rom my home in Long Beach, across Reynolds Channel and beyond the spartina wetlands and white caps of the outer harbor, the New York skyline breaks the horizon's edge. Forever changed since September 11, 2001, the city still exerts a magic pull on me and on the people of the world, for it remains the place of infinite human possibility, the city where every greenhorn can create an American Newness.

Walt Whitman, the wound dresser, would have been proud of New Yorkers during their darkest days after the terrorist attack. I believe his spirit was riding with the crowd on the Brooklyn Ferry when it made its maiden trip across the East River to Manhattan on the first Monday after the tragedy. I was comforted by Whitman's river-crossing poem while standing that day in a crowd of subway riders on the Number Seven train as it rushed under the East River toward Grand Central Station. In the subway tunnel, I felt the pressure of the river water in my ears and stared at my fellow passengers, most of whom originally came from different regions of China, India, Pakistan, and Latin America. "And you that shall cross from shore to shore years hence,"

Whitman wrote, "are more to me, and more in my meditations, than you might suppose . . . what is more subtle than this which ties me to the woman or man that looks into my face, Which fuses me into you now, and pours my meaning into you."

In the period following the disaster, my students expressed a renewed interest in the city's past and especially in what had made it at once a beloved and detested symbol of the American project. The day after the towers fell, I taught a class at Queens College, outside Manhattan, where we struggled to carry on to spite the terrorists. I tried to lighten hearts by describing the first breach of World Trade Center's security, a loving one committed in 1974, just two years after the towers were finished. The French tightrope walker Philippe Petit had evaded the authorities and managed to rig a wire between the towers, a quarter mile up in the sky. New Yorkers on their way to work stared up at him as he dared to cross from one building to the other. That stunt momentarily made the towers seem less grandiose. It was as if the daredevil's silver wire had joined these out-of-scale buildings to an earlier industrial romanticism, to the Brooklyn Bridge, the Statue of Liberty, and the Eiffel Tower.

My fellow catboat lover Captain Prime did not live to see the port face its millennial crisis. Like Rocky Lofaro, who poured the concrete for the towers' foundations, the New York tug captain took pride in the towers' commanding presence. But he also knew that ports are places where disaster often strikes even when all seems calm and routine, just as it did to the victims of the Slocum fire, now the second-worst disaster in the port's history. At any moment a ship can hit a bridge, a plane may fall from the sky, terrorists may strike.

This sense of precariousness is more widely shared now than it was before, but the devotion of New Yorkers to their more vulnerable city is renewed as well. For an increasing number, this devotion means rebuilding the physical city and restoring its natural spaces, the green and blue from which it rises.

For some time, no doubt, it will be more difficult than ever to find a spot along the edge of lower Manhattan to tie up a small boat and loaf along the shore, because who knows what deadly device an innocent-looking craft might carry. But I hope more people will take to the waters of the city to explore the creeks and coves, to ride on the powerful river tides, and to see the city from sea level, where it appears as a place within, and not outside, nature's domain.

Long Beach
September 19, 2001

Bibliography

Auden, W. H. *The Enchafed Flood, or the Romantic Iconography of the Sea.* New York: Random House, 1950.

Beard, John, ed. *Blue Water Views of Old New York.* Barre, Mass.: The Scrimshaw Press, 1970.

Bolster, Jeffrey W. *Black Jacks: African-American Seamen in the Age of Sail.* Cambridge, Mass.: Harvard University Press, 1997.

Bone, Kevin, ed. *The New York Waterfront: Evolution and Building Culture of the Port and Harbor.* New York: The Monacelli Press, 1997.

Bunker, John G. *Harbor and Haven: An Illustrated History of the Port of New York.* Woodland Hills, Calif.: Windsor Publications, 1979.

Caro, Robert A. *The Power Broker: Robert Moses and the Fall of New York.* New York: Alfred A. Knopf, 1974.

Carroll, Lewis. *The Hunting of the Snark, An Agony in Eight Fits.* London: Macmillan and Co., 1876.

Christman, Henry M., ed. *Walt Whitman's New York: From Manhattan to Montauk.* New York: New Amsterdam Books, 1963.

Cudhay, Brian J. *Around Manhattan Island and Other Maritime Tales of New York.* New York: Fordham University Press, 1997.

De Hartag, Jan. *Waters of the New World.* New York: Atheneum, 1961.

Di Donato, Pietro. *Christ in Concrete.* Indianapolis: Bobbs-Merrill, 1939.

DiFazio, William. *The Longshoremen: Community and Resistance on the Brooklyn Waterfront.* South Hadley, Mass.: Bergin and Garvey, 1985.

Dubos, Rene J. *So Human an Animal.* New York: Scribner, 1968.

Grayson, Stan. *Catboats.* 2d ed. Marblehead, Mass.: Devereux Books, 1996.

Hoagland, Edward. *The Tugman's Passage.* New York: Random House, 1982.

Howe, Irving. *The American Newness: Culture and Politics in the Age of Emerson.* Cambridge, Mass.: Harvard University Press, 1986.

Irving, Washington. *Knickerbocker's History of New York.* New York: Doubleday, Doran and Company, 1928.

Kasinitz, Philip, and David Hillyard. "The Old-Timers Tale: The Politics of Nostalgia on the Waterfront," *Journal of Contemporary Ethnography.* 24 (July 1995): pp. 139–64.

Kazin, Alfred. *A Walker in the City.* New York: Harcourt Brace, 1951.

Kieran, John. *A Natural History of New York City.* Boston: Houghton Mifflin, 1959.

Kochiss, John M. *Oystering from New York to Boston.* The American Maritime Library, vol. 7. Middleton, Conn.: Published for Mystic Seaport by Wesleyan University Press, 1974.

Kortchmar, Michael. "New York: An Urban Anchorage," *Yachting*, March 1981, pp. 47ff.

Kwong, Peter. *Forbidden Workers: Illegal Chinese Immigrants and American Labor*. New York: New Press, 1997.

Landow, George. *Images of Crisis: Literary Iconology, 1750 to the Present*. Boston: Routledge and Kegan Paul, 1982.

Lear, Edward. *A Book of Bosh*. Harmondsworth, G.B.: Puffin Books, 1975.

Leavens, John M., ed. *The Catboat Book*. New York: McGraw Hill Professional Publishing, 1991.

Leopold, Aldo. *A Sand County Almanac*. New York, Oxford University Press, 1949.

Liebling, A. J. *Back Where I Come From: New York*. New York: Sheridan House, 1938.

Lydon, James G. *Pirates, Privateers, and Profits*. Upper Saddle River, N.J.: Gregg Press, 1970.

Mitchell, Joseph. *Up in the Old Hotel and Other Stories*. New York: Pantheon Books, 1992.

Morris, Jan. *The Great Port: A Passage through New York*. New York: Oxford University Press, 1969.

Perec, George. *Ellis Island*. Paris: P.O.L., 1995.

Rattray, Jeanette Edwards. *Perils of the Port of New York: Maritime Disasters from Sandy Hook to Execution Rocks*. New York: Dodd, Mead, 1973.

Rogers, Elizabeth Barlow. *The Forests and Wetlands of New York City*. Boston: Little Brown, 1971.

Seitz, Sharon, and Stuart Miller. *The Other Islands of New York*

City: A Historical Companion. Woodstock, Vt.: Countryman Press, 1996.

Stapleton, Laurence, ed. *Henry David Thoreau: A Writer's Journal.* New York: Dover Publications, 1960.

Tanacredi, John T. *Gateway, A Visitor's Companion.* Mechanicsburg, Pa.: Stackpole Books, 1963.

Teal, John. *Life and Death of the Salt Marsh.* Boston: Little Brown, 1969.

Thomas, Lewis. *Lives of a Cell: Notes of a Biology Watcher.* New York: Viking Press, 1974.

Thoreau, Henry David. *Cape Cod.* Boston: Houghton, Mifflin, 1893.

Trachtenberg, Alan. *Brooklyn Bridge Fact and Symbol* (2d ed.). Chicago: University of Chicago Press, 1979.

Waldman, John. *Heartbeats in the Muck: A Dramatic Look at the History, Sea Life, and Environment of New York Harbor.* New York: Lyons Press, 1999.

White, E. B. *An E. B. White Reader.* New York: Harper and Row, 1966.

Wilkinson, Alec. *The Riverkeeper.* New York: Vintage Books, 1992.

Wilson, Edward Osborne. *Sociobiology.* Cambridge, Mass.: Harvard University Press, 1975.